ENERGY
NEVER
DIES

T0097903

ENERGY NEVER DIES

AFRO-OPTIMISM AND CREATIVITY IN CHICAGO

AYANA CONTRERAS

UNIVERSITY OF ILLINOIS PRESS
Urbana, Chicago, and Springfield

© 2021 by the Board of Trustees
of the University of Illinois
All rights reserved
1 2 3 4 5 C P 5 4 3 2 1
∞ This book is printed on acid-free paper.

Library of Congress Cataloging-in-Publication Data
Names: Contreras, Ayana, 1981– author.
Title: Energy never dies : Afro-optimism and creativity in
    Chicago / Ayana Contreras.
Description: Urbana : University of Illinois Press, 2021. | Includes
    bibliographical references and index.
Identifiers: LCCN 2021035774 (print) | LCCN 2021035775 (ebook)
    | ISBN 9780252044069 (cloth) | ISBN 9780252086113
    (paperback) | ISBN 9780252053009 (ebook)
Subjects: LCSH: African Americans—Illinois—Chicago—Music—
    History and criticism. | Popular music—Illinois—Chicago—
    Music—History and criticism. | African Americans—
    Illinois—Chicago—Social life and customs. | African
    Americans—Illinois—Chicago—Attitudes.
Classification: LCC ML3479 .c64 2021 (print) | LCC ML3479
    (ebook) | DDC 780.8996073/11—dc23
LC record available at https://lccn.loc.gov/2021035774
LC ebook record available at https://lccn.loc.gov/2021035775

This book is dedicated to my grandmother Phyllis, who believed in me, to all of the wonderful folks who've been so generous with their stories, their old record albums, and their time, and most of all to the Black Chicagoans of our past who had the audacity to believe our future could be brighter than even they could imagine.

CONTENTS

THE VERGE OF SPRING
OPTIMISM IN BLACK CHICAGO

If you really want to be free, you have to take
charge of your capacity to shape the world.

Kerry James Marshall

I am preoccupied with stories. Not fairy tales, not imaginings, but real-life stories that give me hope in the improbable. It just happens to be that Black Chicago is a place steeped in those stories. Unfortunately, much of today's media about Black Chicago paints the community as a soulless, lawless place where brother is pitted against brother. Those stories zoom in on the few. The many are rendered silent. Bit players in their own movie.

If you are not from here, some stories might be unknown to you; but to explain the meaning of Taurus Flavors or Curtis Mayfield in a line or two would do a disservice to all of us.

I believe that Black Chicago has a unique culture, rooted in self-determination, creativity, optimism, and hustle. It's passed down through our music and media, replicated over and over. And that music and media has been disseminated throughout the world, via Haki Madhubuti's Third World Press, *Ebony* and *Jet* magazines, the work of Lerone Bennett Jr., Curtom, Chess, and Brunswick Records, and even through Afro Sheen advertisements on *Soul Train*. And that's the short list.

Curator Leslie Guy (a Philadelphia native who at one time worked at Chicago's DuSable Museum of African American History) once told me that Black Chicago feels like "it is always on the verge of spring," as though that big breakthrough, that metaphoric flush of sunshine, is always just around the corner.

I argue that part of that feeling is due to our trait of clinging fast to our faith. Baked into the culture of Black Chicago is the belief that the improbable can happen, perhaps against the odds, because there are so many tales of these things happening right before our eyes. In the world of visual art, you needn't look further than the intergalactic career arc of Kerry James Marshall or the equally lofty launch of artist and urban planner Theaster Gates, both Chicagoans. Marshall has called Chicago home for decades, and Gates was born and raised in Chicago. Their success stories alone have brought innumerable members of the creative class to Chicago. But the part of those oft-cited fairy tales that is often left out is how long each of them toiled on the edge of winter before their breakthrough to their spring. Each of them are incredibly willful souls, and part of their successes lie within their shared belief that they can craft their own narrative.

I choose to pepper this text with the term "Afro-optimism" to describe this phenomenon, primarily as an antithesis to Afro-pessimism: a concept to which I have a visceral reaction each time I encounter it.

Usually traced back to Orlando Patterson's 1982 book, *Slavery and Social Death*, the concept of Afro-pessimism identifies slavery as the perpetual state of being for Black America. That we are, in essence, doomed as a consequence of birth.

As recently as 2020, Frank B. Wilderson III argued a version of this notion in his book *Afropessimism*. "For Wilderson, the state of slavery, for Black people, is permanent," Vinson Cunningham explains. He continues: "every Black person is always a slave and, therefore, a perpetual corpse, buried beneath the world and stinking it up."[1]

This lens speaks so ardently to the scars, the trauma of slavery, but in my estimation it also does a disservice to those who literally passed through the nadir so that we might come out the other side. And let's say, for argument's sake, that the vestiges of slavery in fact forms the basis of Black American culture. Does that imply that the frame of self-defeatism, of never-ending tailspin, is an imperative of viewing Blackness?

It's noteworthy to me that Wilderson's book *Afropessimism* folds vignettes of his life into the argument. Looking at the plain facts of his upbringing and accomplishments (his father was a professor, Wilderson earned a bachelor's degree from Dartmouth College, a master's from Columbia University, and a PhD from UC Berkeley, and Wilderson III is an accomplished dramatist, writer, and educator in his own right): his life could just as easily be framed as a tome on Afro-optimism. That is to say that despite being constantly Otherized and ostracized, he has crafted a life to be proud of. But he chooses to concentrate on the factors (systemic and otherwise) that hang as a specter over him—let's call them the external facts of Blackness. I don't suggest in *Energy Never Dies* that these external facts of Blackness don't exist, or should be addressed and accounted for, I suggest that they cannot extinguish the wonderous stuff we are made of: the internal facts of Blackness.

To me, this lens of Afro-pessimism (as expressed by Wilderson and many others) quite literally counters the lifeblood, the very DNA of Black Chicago culture. If the Johnsons had not believed in the notion of a Black version of *Life* magazine, *Ebony* magazine would have never existed. Black Chicago is defined by self-determination and by the belief in the improbable. We believe that, despite reports to the contrary, we are not yet dead, but perhaps as curator Leslie Guy surmised, we are on the verge of spring. If our Black American ancestors had not believed in the possibility of a better tomorrow (in order to just keep living), I shudder to think of what the world would have missed out on. Self-defeatism is easy to get sucked up into, but belief in an alternate reality is the escape hatch (if only in our own minds).

In an unpublished essay written during a 2007 visit to Chicago, philosopher, poet, and theorist Fred Moten writes:

> My optimism, black optimism, is bound up with what it is to claim blackness and the appositional, runaway black operations that have been thrust upon it. The burden, the constraint, is the aim, the paradoxically aleatory goal that animates escape in and the possibility of escape from.[2]

He goes on to conjure up a Folkways recording, "Da Da Da Da," by the Child Development Group of Mississippi: "Here is one such black op. I play this in appreciation for being in Chicago, which is everybody's sweet home, everybody's land of California, as Robert Johnson puts it. This is music from a Head Start program in Mississippi in the mid-sixties and as you all know Chicago is a city in Mississippi, Mississippi a (fugue) state of mind in Chicago." Commenting on the children singing on the 1967 recording, Moten clarifies:

> These children are the voices of the future in the past, the voices of the future in our present. In this recording, this remainder, their fugitivity, remains, for me, in the intensity of their refrain, of their straining against constraint, cause for the optimism they perform.

Moten's repeated reference to escape refers to his idea that Blackness is fugitive, that it functions outside of the borders and mores of mainstream society, like the Mexican pirate radio stations of the twentieth century that exploited that country's broadcast standards to blast their signals across the border with little regard to the FCC.

A notable complication to the term "Afro-optimism" is its use as a lens of postcolonial African studies. Ebere Onwudiwe and Minabere Ibelema-by's 2002 edited volume, *Afro-Optimism: Perspectives on Africa's Advances*, asserts that the view of Africa as a forsaken, war-ridden land is intrinsically flawed, and that such negative attitudes can be traced back to "European slave traders [who] promoted and exploited the lore of a primitive and foreboding Africa as a defense of the primitive and inhuman trade." The editors say at the outset that "[their] goal is to tell Africa's other story, to make the cases that Africa's other successes to date are bases for a hopeful future if detrimental internal tendencies and external factors are reversed."[3]

This only enriches the definition of Afro-optimism as applied to Black Americans. The goal that Onwudiwe and Ibelemaby express is in fact a primary goal of the Black Arts Movement, of its precursor, Negritude, and more broadly, articulates the implicit goal of so much of the rich culture born in Black Chicago. To illustrate the necessity of positive expressions of Blackness, the authors even invoked of the Reverend Jesse Jackson's rallying cry of "I Am Somebody" (a key slice of classic Afro-optimism if ever there was one).[4] This invocation not only affirms the Pan-African connective tissue of the term Afro-optimism, but it illustrates a certain cultural capital that is as vital now as it ever was.

Speaking with Naomi Beckwith (then the Museum of Contemporary Art Chicago's Manilow Senior Curator) about the trajectory of her career, we hit upon why she returned to Chicago from New York City—arguably the center of the American art world.

I chose to come back. Yeah, it's funny. I was having a really good time in New York. My career was going great. I still have some of the best friends of my life there. But I wanted to come back to my hometown.

People always ask if family brought me back, and yeah, of course the answer is yes. The immediate blood family brought me back. But there's also a bigger sense of family in Chicago that was really important to me.

There's a sense that Black people must work together to accomplish things. That despite whatever differences you have: socioeconomically, what differences you may have in terms of national origin, what differences you may even have in terms of professional affiliation, people in Chicago have the ability to band together and get stuff done.

I'm thinking definitely about our political abilities. It took a while [*chuckles*] but . . . we elected a very effective Black mayor in the '80s [Harold Washington]. We, of course, created the first Black president in the US. But I'm also thinking about these Black utopian spaces in Chicago that sprouted up, especially around Johnson Publishing Company, or the DuSable Museum.

The Black community in Chicago has been so invested in cultural practice and political practice in a way that makes Black sociality here in Chicago incredibly rich and incredibly important.[5]

This is how some of the stories of Black Chicago operate. The physical vestiges of these stories, the spoils, might be long gone or dismantled. But the legend, long since rendered down to its most essential spirit, lives on. We speak them into existence. We conjure up their energy to fuel our futures.

This is the thing. The Chicago Thing that I hope to God that we regain. In the twentieth century, Black Chicago caught the proverbial tiger by the tail, and shaped our narrative around the world. Despite crippling injustice, we sent out messages about Black people imbued with buoyant hopes. Even during Jim Crow, the *Chicago Defender* beckoned Black folk northward with promises of a better life. A job in a factory. A home. And in the wake of the passing of the Civil Rights Act of 1964, we took those messages even further. As Curtis Mayfield implored,

Move on Up!
Towards your destination!
Remember your dream
It's your only scheme
So keep on Pushin'[6]

Historically, many of Black Chicago's messages are linked to economic empowerment. Chicago-based *Ebony* magazine told us in 1971 of a collective of enterprising Elton, Louisiana, housewives who got their home-sewn dashikis sold in Sears stores (through their cooperative initiative, Eltwear).[7] An accompanying photo shows Mrs. Edna Mae Woods with an assortment of garments draped across her outstretched forearms. Her young daughter, Maxine, stands in the foreground holding a brown hand-made rag doll, braided pigtails tied in fat yarn bows.

So many messages, and their accompanying images, still resonate with us right now. Today's generation of Black Chicagoans, in particular, are deeply inspired by them. As an indirect consequence, a new Black Renaissance akin to the Black Arts Movement of the late 1960s is afoot in Chicago.

I want us to never lose sight that we are the masters of our narrative and, thus, our destiny. We've suffered a slow erosion in Black mass media in the city, with various record labels shuttering and with *Ebony*'s editorial operations moving to California.

If we don't cling to what makes us stronger, I fear we'll succumb to what aims to break us apart.

I am a DJ because I believe that there is power in gathering together and listening and even dancing. I am a radio maker because I believe in the power of sharing our stories. And I have written this book because I believe in the power of Black Chicago. In us.

This book traces that power, that energy as it has flowed between generations.

My grandmother Phyllis Flowers inadvertently named this book one night at her South Side kitchen table. She told me she was dying, and as I reeled silently at that news, she told me she'd been grappling with the news for a while. Her thoughts teetered to the philosophical.

She said, "Energy never dies."

I know that to be true. I know that I am her in so many ways. She taught me implicitly to be fearless. To believe in my own power. To navigate the world without regrets. To cultivate my creativity. To harvest my joy.

So many of the stories of *Energy Never Dies* are about how generations (and even cultural artifacts) in Black Chicago are in conversation with one another. And this flow of energy plays an absolutely crucial role in maintaining our connection to a beautiful narrative that we can be proud of.

I am particularly interested in how the transfer of these traditions transpired during the post–civil rights era. A moment when Black Chicago's culture was conduit and midwife to new, bold messages of Blackness that were disseminated across the nation and world via our media: our music, our periodicals, and even through television.

My goal with this book was to build a narrative primarily using my personally acquired archive of mostly ephemeral materials: newsletters, liner notes, magazines, event programs, recorded music, press releases, and advertisements. I also conducted dozens of interviews, both on my radio show, *Reclaimed Soul*, and privately that are collected here. Still other elements were initially published on my blog, Darkjive.com. This book very intentionally draws from nonacademic sources. That's because I wanted to tell this story using mass media materials that were generally accessible and that were immediate, unfiltered cultural artifacts of their day to explore how these ideas interfaced with the world.

Powerful messages of "Beautiful people use Afro Sheen" and that the improbable is possible are within Black Chicago's very marrow. And they are passed on through improbably true tales, and through physical artifacts that still clutch the power of Black alchemy. And they echo in the work being created this very moment in Black Chicago.

I only hope my words do it justice.

ON STONY ISLAND AVENUE

BOULEVARD OF BLACK CULTURE

Creativity is a holy thing in Black Chicago. Creativity and belief in the impossible. And creativity is astounding, powerfully churning, just beneath the surface of everything around us, waiting for a fissure (or a faithful messenger) to aid in its escape. And it is the story of that unique creative energy, which renews itself as it transfers from generation to generation, that quickens my pulse.

I find evidence of this in stoic buildings, and I find evidence in vinyl records: testaments to dreams and beliefs. In identity, in possibility, in power (despite oppression). The buildings root the story in a very concrete place. The records lend to the story a sensation of humanity, of heart and of soul.

So where does the story begin?

At 79th Street and Stony Island Avenue? The cantilevered Chicago Skyway rises above, casting a noirish shadow over a bustling six-point intersection. A whitewashed, abandoned Leon's BBQ is to my right. Not even twenty years ago, Leon Finney Sr. would shuttle between his kingdom of barbecue shacks in his beige Rolls-Royce (license plate "LEON RIB").[1]

Near the northwest corner of the intersection, a nondescript whitewashed storefront once housed Clarence Ludd's High Chaparral club, one of the most popular clubs of the 1970s. The High Chaparral hosted the who's who of local and national talent from Tyrone Davis to B.B. King. Those days are long gone.

The New Regal Theater sits to my left. The blonde-bricked theater glitters with multicolored faux-Moorish ceramic tiles. According to lore, the architect, John Eberson, was inspired by an ornate Persian incense burner he found in New Orleans.

In the 1980s, the theater, originally known as the Avalon, was purchased by Ed and Bettianne Gardner (who had made a fortune in the Black hair-care business with their Soft Sheen products).

Ed and Bettianne's objective was to create a space for Black creativity to flourish. In a 1987 article, Ed stated, "We feel the black community has got an instrument that can really continue to make life better, that's the purpose of this theater to bring entertainment, bring quality of life up, and encourage our youngsters."[2]

The Avalon was renamed in 1987 to reclaim the splendor of the original Regal Theater, which stood some miles away in Bronzeville before its 1968 closure. The axis of the Black South Side of Chicago had shifted farther south beginning in the late 1950s, and this was jeweled proof of the shift. Who knew that that shift would also mark a peak of sorts? The beginning of a molasses-slow decline?

Despite a marked decline around it, the New Regal is still standing at 79th and Stony. Just north of what was Curtis Mayfield's Curtom Records. Just east of the massive old Sears and Roebuck building, vacated after ninety years in the neighborhood. Just south of Mosque Maryam, where Louis Farrakhan speaks on Sundays to the faithful of the Nation of Islam. In fact, the bow-tied Muslim men in suits selling bean pies are as much of a landmark at the intersection of 79th and Stony as is the New Regal.

Perhaps a victim of repeated turnover in ownership, the New Regal Theater has never truly lived up to its namesake in terms of relevance in the community. A lovely jeweled white elephant of a music box. Silent. Dormant. Yet it is a metaphor for the struggle of Black Chicago. A struggle often articulated by young Black creatives. Faithful messengers. It's a struggle rooted in the belief and faith in our collective resurrection.

And, it is no coincidence that just north of the mosque on Stony Island rises Theaster Gates's Stony Island Arts Bank. This is a contemporary art gallery, event space, community center, and archive. Gates has called it "redemptive architecture." The 1923 cloud-white bank building, girded by tall classical columns, had been abandoned since the 1980s. Theaster noted in a 2015 interview that "projects like this require belief more than they require funding."[3] It is by no coincidence that one of the Arts Bank's permanent collections is the record collection of Frankie Knuckles. Even before his premature death, Frankie had obtained mythical status for his contributions as a DJ and producer during the golden age of house music in Chicago (beginning about in the early 1980s). It's a body of materials that carries immeasurable weight in the community, and suspends disbelief in the power of culture to change the world.

Black Chicago is populated not just by people, but also by physical objects that are testaments to periods of forward momentum. Objects and places that are still imbued with the power to inspire and to instill a swell of pride.

But as these objects inevitably break down, what remains to tell the story transcribed on liner notes and found photographs? And what becomes of the pride and possibility that trickled down from the Soft Sheen mansion to the Henry Horner Homes?

Thinking about what we choose to save and what we throw away intrigues me. What will become of ephemeral objects that never make the digital leap from paper to pixel or from groove to gigabyte? What bits of knowledge live on these physical artifacts, beyond their native media? And what happens when these formats degrade? Much of the corporal proof of our creative capital is in the midst of a breakdown. But the spirit remains.

Jawole Willa Jo Zollar stated to an audience in 2014 that she admired Chicago's Black arts community, in particular our spirit of "Black radical imagination." Her eyes glimmered with palpable energy. Zollar, founder of the dance troupe Urban Bush Women, was in Chicago that spring as part of an artists' residency with Columbia College Chicago's Dance Department.[4]

Months later, I recounted her statement to lifelong Chicagoan and free jazz saxophonist David Boykin over a vegan meal at a Hyde Park restaurant. We wondered aloud what she had meant. What was this uniquely Chicago thing?

I sighed as two middle-aged Black men slipped out of the booth beside us, one holding a dog-eared paperback copy of *The Destruction of Black*

Civilization by Chancellor Williams. The book has been in print through Chicago's Third World Press since 1974. It holds a prominent place on bookshelves across Black Chicago and has served as a sort of Black nationalist–thought gateway drug for younger generations here.

The Third World Press describes the book as "intended to be a general rebellion against the subtle message from even the most 'liberal' white authors (and their Negro disciples): 'You belong to a race of nobodies. You have no worthwhile history to point to with pride.'"[5]

Yes. *That* is the unspoken Chicago thing. A mind state tied to a place where improbably huge stories happen, bound by segregation. The thing that allows for an amazingly rich legacy of strong Black business and creativity. The basinet for free jazz, modern gospel, and the electrified blues. Later for a striding, larger-than-life brand of soul, and even house music. That Chicago thing produced literary behemoths like Lorraine Hansberry, Gwendolyn Brooks, and Richard Wright, and is still producing fruit like Eve Ewing and Nate Marshall. *Ebony*, *Jet*, the *Chicago Defender*, and Third World Press put the good news, the Black radical gospel, in print. Generations of visual artists like Nick Cave, Kerry James Marshall, and Richard Hunt continue to push boundaries.

And today, a new breed of artists, academics, and cultural workers is working to fashion arts creation hubs that dually build upon an arts-based economic model and an ethos of creative reuse.

One thread is a loosely bound constellation of projects sort of orbiting around the work of Theaster Gates; but it is real, and in the present day, and has inspired a small-scale Black artists migration to Chicago.

Though a variety of jobs and physical goods have been born out of these projects, in my opinion, the chief product is an overarching swell of pride felt in spaces that had once been forlorn. Pride tied to the improbable coming to pass in a community that stands to gain the most.

Theaster once noted to me that it was Chicago that allowed his art practice to achieve the scope that it has. The space is here. "In space there is opportunity," he shared. In space, there is the ultimate raw material.

But comparing him to titans of industry like George and Joan Johnson would be in error. His goal has never been to build long-term businesses; rather, his model revolves around extended pop-up enterprises that showcase what could be. He is an artist, first and foremost, who works under the hypothesis that we have more underutilized capital (creative and physical) in Black Chicago than even we sometimes realize. This space exists in concentrations because much of Chicago is hemmed in by segregation. Yet, within occasionally painful constraints, amazingly free transformative ideas have transpired.

In a place so bereft of large-scale development, Theaster's high-profile projects can appear as hollow baubles: beautifully crafted spaces that don't seem to address the trauma in surrounding neighborhoods. But that critique assumes that spaces for art, spaces that celebrate culture, aren't as important to the health of a community as a place to get clothes drycleaned. The hierarchy of needs comes into play, but certainly the arts have a role in overall quality of life, a truth played out by other creative reuse–based projects like Rick Lowe's Project Row Houses in Houston, or even St. Elmo Village in Los Angeles, a grouping of buildings that were originally silent film star Mary Pickford's horse stables. The complex was converted in 1969 by artists Roderick and Rozzell Sykes into an arts space for creatives of all ages.

One episode of the TV program *Black Omnibus*, hosted by James Earl Jones and shot in Los Angeles in 1972, featured Rozzell Sykes and the children of St. Elmo Village as well as Paul Mooney and the Bar-Kays (outfitted in baby blue and in town for *Wattstax*). Sykes explained to Jones, that since the building of the complex, in the surrounding community, "There has been a harvest of awakening. The streets of St. Elmo that used to be drab and brown are now green."[6]

But back to the term "Black radical imagination," a phrase as mysterious and obtuse as the cosmos. What exactly is this thing? The phrase is credited to Robin D. G. Kelley from his 2002 *Freedom Dreams: The Black Radical Imagination*. In many ways, imagination is the ability to push past the concrete and into the realm of the marvelous. In the book, Kelley further defines the marvelous:

> My mother taught us that the Marvelous was free—in the patterns of a stray bird feather, in a Hudson River sunset, in the view from our fire escape, in the stories she told us, in the way she sang Gershwin's "Summertime," in a curbside rainbow created by the alchemy of motor oil and water from an open hydrant.[7]

Akin to the marvelous, Black radical imagination, to me, is the elevation of what could be considered mundane. The Bible says that "faith is the substance of things hoped for, the evidence of things not seen."[8] Perhaps, folding faith into the pot of imagination (with a bit of speculation) is what this Chicago brand of Black radical imagination is all about. It is Afro-optimism laced with self-determination, an unwavering belief in the possibility of tomorrow.

Kelley's book focuses on examples of revolutionary artists and intellectuals, many of whom are known mostly in rarefied circles of Academia. But in Chicago, that Black radical imagination has had very practical, community-based actualizations. For example, there's Black radical religion, which includes a number of religious groups that have had radical, pro-Black slants on social issues that have plagued our communities. Those smartly suited men selling bean pies and the *Final Call* (a Nation of Islam–owned newspaper) at 79th Street and Stony Island Avenue radiate with a pride palpable to Black people only peripherally connected to Mosque Maryam down the street. In decades past, the Moorish temple reflected an overarching desire for deeper knowledge of our pre-American history. Drew Ali (founder of the Moorish Science Temples) told us we descended from the Moors, and that slave owners had worked to suppress our true heritage. Today, only a specter of the Moorish temples remain.

Then, there's the Afro-optimism that girds entrepreneurship in Black Chicago: so, intertwined with the history of Black Power and Black arts here in Chicago, that there's no way to speak of one without the others. Businesses that brought us pride through their mere existence. Barbecue baron Leon Finney Sr. in his beige Rolls-Royce was an expression of audacious possibility. Black Chicago businesses created buildings tantamount to pyramids like the Soft Sheen mansion in Chatham and the Ebony/Jet building at 820 South Michigan Avenue. Black entrepreneurs gambled on art and music. Black businesses have fought to tell our story. Today, the Ebony/Jet high-rise is populated by condos, a cream concrete behemoth that was once chock-full of mid-century modern delights. Yet the building (which was also designed by a Black architect) still holds the power to make Black Chicago's blood coarse with pride.

Across generations in Black Chicago, there have been a series of struggles to build artistic autonomy and venues for arts presentations. That includes a concerted effort in the 1970s to build a "soul center" in Chicago. It was an artistic-entrepreneurial marriage, to be sure. It was a push to truly own *the music*: that gumbo of soul, gospel, jazz, and blues that is our birthright. And, in many ways, "the music," which is usually uttered in half-whispered tones, is the most ubiquitous form of uniquely Black Chicago Culture. The music is *everyone's*. It hums at AP Deli, a takeout corned-beef spot on East 75th Street. It wails from a radio at a barber shop. A patchwork chorus sings along to a favorite verse. We take ownership. But, I am concerned that, sometimes, this heritage is taken for granted. The specificity of names and release dates and stories tend to fade through the filtering of years.

Guglielmo Marconi believed that radio waves did not decay, that they traveled across space and time forever, and if a strong enough receiver could be built, we could pick up every radio wave that ever was. But that is not so. Without intentional documentation, bits and pieces of our heritage are in danger of degrading. And specificities are in danger of fading to static.

That is a particular shame, because our ancestors worked hard to build a canon of creativity that we can be supremely proud of.

A former coworker, a lifelong Black Chicagoan, once said to me that she wished Black Chicagoans had a "culture." We were eating brightly colored *paletas*, or Mexican Popsicles. She compared Black Chicagoans' culture to that of Mexican American Chicagoans. Ironically, she said it one summer Saturday as we strolled through Jackson Park, surrounded by family reunions pumping Chicago-bred soul music. Lustrous red and blue balloons swayed in the lake breeze. Older folks were teaching a couple of the young ones to step, a particularly Chicago couple dance.

After she rattled off barbecue shacks and fast-food spots as things we ought to be ashamed of, I gathered she meant that she wished we had a "culture" that would cause a swell of pride.

Sometimes, we can't see the forest for the trees. But, if she knew what those barbecue shacks represent (beyond the smoke and the bulletproof glass) and how they are a uniquely Chicago phenomenon, perhaps she'd feel differently. In the mid-twentieth century, barbecue shacks sprouted up and spread across the South and West Sides of Chicago, but a few names in particular were elevated to legend: Lems, Leon's, and the Collins Brothers.

The smoke, to me, is incense emanating from mammoth, boxy, glass-and-steel aquarium smokers like the one at Lem's BBQ on 75th Street. The smoke rises slowly, coiling serpentine above the asphalt and concrete. At night, the smoke is blue-black magic obscuring candy-colored, big-bodied American cars: drop-top Eldorados, Caprice Classics, and Rivieras with gleaming rims and white-on-white interiors. The smell alone is a miraculous thing. And the legendary yarns spun about the proprietors are but another facet of that miracle.

Leon Finney's creamy-tan Rolls-Royce, parked out front of his barbecue joint in the late 1990s, was by far the first Rolls I ever saw (outside of those on television). Lem's BBQ is an anchor on 75th Street. The business opened back in 1951.

Argia B. Collins's Mumbo Sauce (a different sauce altogether from the Mumbo Sauce of Washington, DC) was one of the first Black-owned products to advertise in *Life* magazine. The 1970 ad featured a smiling Argia B. in front of a backyard barbecue pit, magic wand in one hand, bottle of Mumbo Sauce in the other. The copy declared "Meal Magic from the Barbecue King."[9]

Thoughts of how barbecue built little economic engines remind me of the resourcefulness of Black Chicago, but it was okra that electrified me. Seeing a bowl of okra—not in Chicago as I'd known it, but in Cuba in 2017—galvanized what had been simmering beneath my skin.

Okra made the transatlantic journey on slave ships alongside human cargo. The fact that the fuzzy green seed-laden vegetable is eaten by Black folk in the United States is a miracle. A vegetable umbilical cord.

For a moment one summer, I was hooked on fried okra in greasy brown sacks from Laurence's Fisheries, a long-standing fish shack on Cermak and Canal in Chicago.

We, my Black kin, were not supposed to survive. And yet here we are. We are our ancestors' wildest dreams. And yet, here too is okra. (And yams. And black-eyed peas. And all manner of celebratory red drinks, but that's another tale.) Feeding our souls.

Still, seeing the okra in Cuba, in a bowl hewn from a gourd, with a banana leaf serving as a tablecloth took my breath away, like seeing a friend from a past life. We were visiting a rural community in the hills above Baracoa, and they had put out an amazing spread of lovingly made food.

She was crying. One of the brown ladies in the large hut where we'd gathered. A rooster strutted across the dirt floor. I looked in her eyes and knew we were thinking the same thought.

I said, "Mi familia."

We embraced.

She pointed to a nearby line of the men from her family. Our family. One after another they embraced me and kissed me on my cheek. She repeated "Tu hermano . . . tu hermano . . . tu hermano" (Your brother . . . your brother . . . your brother). And it was true. Though I'm not from Cuba, I was at home.

I had been to Ghana two years before. The only moment I felt someone reach out to me in Ghana was in Cape Coast, at the foot of a huge whitewashed slave castle where captive Africans were held and ultimately loaded on slave ships. A light honey-brown woman with freckles saw my similarly tinted brown skin and approached me. She smiled and said, "We are the same." It was the archetypal homecoming moment that so many Black Americans travel to Africa in search of.

That is, until my guide pointed toward the woods. He said that the woman was from a village where the slavers had kept concubines. Her light honey-brown skin was a product of that legacy. As a Black woman, I knew that, likely, the hue of my skin that caused me to be seen as Other in sub-Saharan Africa was likely also due at least in part to some shameful exploitation in my lineage.

But, in Ghana, I never felt what I felt in Cuba. This was a very particular shared narrative. A reaffirmation of resilience: tied not to shame, but to overcoming. A shared story of family. A story of connections.

I had come to Cuba a week earlier as part of a cultural exchange, primarily to play music with musicians there. Our group stayed in coastal towns: first Santiago de Cuba, then Guantánamo, then Baracoa.

I brought with me my twenty-three-key mbira, also known as a kalimba, sanza, or a thumb piano. I had fallen in love with the sound of the instrument through old Earth, Wind & Fire records. In fact, Maurice White, lead singer of Earth, Wind & Fire (who was a Chicagoan) dubbed his production company Kalimba.

My mbira is essentially a rectangular piece of wood with two strips of flat steel keys affixed to the wood with metal wire. Well over a thousand years old, the instrument is found in various iterations across Africa. My mbira was made in Zimbabwe.

It was important for me to bring my mbira because of its relationship to the Cuban marimbula. As I was packing for my trip, somehow, I had

9

remembered that Cubans employ the marimbula in a lot of traditional music (like changui and rhumba). The instrument consists of a hollow wooden box, often large enough to sit on. It has a large round cutout in the front with a row of fingerlike flat steel strips or keys. The family resemblance of the mbira and marimbula is stunning, both visually and sonically.

Even the names "mbira" and "marimbula" imply a clear kinship. And grizzled brown musicians invariably approached me and asked about my instrument.

I had my elevator pitch ready:

Mbira: Emmeh-Beh-Eh. . . . Sí. From Zimbabwe. Sí. Escuche [*pluck-pluck-pluck*]. Yes. Familia. Es el abuelo [grandad] de la maribula. Ha ha ha ha.

My Spanish is pretty rough.

They immediately smiled. None had ever seen this thing. Yet, somehow, we were all bound to it, as the metal tines were bound to the wood. It was a beautiful feeling of connection.

The mbira's tuning is idiosyncratic, and certainly not connected to any Western tonal scale. Somehow, it was always in tune with what the Cuban musicians were playing. I favor playing the mbira as a tonal rhythmic instrument in 6 or 8 time, but with the Cubans I began to employ rhythms that laced around the clave, another African transplant.

The clave is something that is hard to explain because to call it a rhythm is an oversimplification of its beauty.

It is a five-beat rhythmic structure that is the backbone of many Latin music forms. It is sometimes played explicitly on wooden sticks called claves, but the clave is also sometimes implied, or played around as a guidepost. The Spanish word *clave* literally translates as "key."

Bip-Bop-Bop [*pause*] Bip-Bop [*pause*]

But the clave exists in traditional Black American idioms, too. We call it the hambone. A traditional children's song called "Hambone" was recorded by Chicago bandleader Red Saunders for Okeh Records in 1952. The recording is amazing in that it captures the beat, the energy of the children's chant (credited as the Hambone Kids). "Hambone" is also amazing because it is a clear ancestor to the percolating house music rhythms that would emanate from Chicago three decades later.

Some folks also know the clave or hambone as the Bo Diddley beat.

Bo was born in Mississippi and grew up on the South Side of Chicago. He utilized his square-bodied cherry-red guitar to play the Hambone beat in signature songs like 1956's "Who Do You Love?" (released on Chicago's Chess Records). The beat has clear ties to sub-Saharan Africa and was executed as part of the juba dance here in the United States. The stomping and slapping of the juba served as a rhythmic guidepost for slave musicians as they played music. African drums were outlawed on most plantations, so the musicians used their bodies to keep time.

Notably, Bo Diddley's stage name is reminiscent of the diddley bow, which is a single-stringed guitar-like instrument that used to be popular in the rural American South. It's generally homemade, and also has ties to West Africa.

The levels of connections are incredibly robust.

Once home from Cuba, stirring a pot of mustard greens, I was ruminating on the clave, and okra, and mbira, and family. I thought about just how many connections exist despite so many intentions for those ties to be extinguished. Centuries ago we were stripped of our names, punished severely from using our languages, and not able to follow our indigenous spiritual practices.

Some of us were taught to undervalue our culture.

We were not immigrants by choice. And every vestige of our culture that we were able to hang onto was hard won.

Yet, so many elements survived: sometimes remixed, sometimes hiding in plain sight. In so many ways, we are so clearly connected to a global Black cultural narrative. That spirit of the remix, of optimistic imagination, lives and thrives in Chicago (despite hardships). We remixed and electrified the Delta Blues, broadcasting the results across the globe. We added a new twist to barbecue. And generation after generation, the dreams of the Great Migration of Blacks from the deep south to Chicago are reborn.

SORT OF A DREAM

THE SOUTHERN SENSIBILITY AND FLOW OF CHICAGO'S WEST SIDE

Black Americans are grapefruits. Hear me out on this.

In the beginning, in the Garden of Eden, I suppose, there was the genus citrus. Let's say all of us Black folk stemmed from there. Today at your local grocery store, a shopper is likely to see a grapefruit alongside a banana and imagine that the world has always known this plump, ripe fruit . . . full of flavorful juice, sweet yet sour.

But in reality, grapefruits are a hybrid of dubious, unplanned origin. It was first described in the late eighteenth century, a creole fruit found in the New World. We know that they are genetically citrus, and that they're derived from the pomelo and the sweet orange (itself a hybrid fruit), but that's where it gets fuzzy. By the looks of things, we are pomelo, presumably, but not precisely. Nigerian? Perhaps. Malian? Conceivably. We are Black, but somehow not precisely African. What is certain is that we are a commodity, our bodies splayed out for consumption. Our juice, our joie de vivre, constantly harvested.

Sometimes I feel as though I'm uncommonly perishable. Like my lips are made of fruit flesh, skin like a grapefruit segment, just waiting to tear. The thought builds, and I imagine I'm on a collision course for unnamed doom: a villainous breakdown. Then I wake up.

I realize it's only sort of a dream.

Everything is passing away (peeling away like citrus skin), a breath away from death. Man comforts himself with the idea of "archiving." Archiving assumes victory over death. We die anyway, though selected remnants remain.

What we save may last forever, but it may prove to be absolutely useless to the future. At least in its present state. Or the medium may rot in wait, leaving scarcely a fragrance behind.

Around the time of Chicago's storied blizzard of 1967—which dumped twenty-three inches of snow over the course of about thirty-five hours—out in San Francisco, the first "Human Be-In" (or "Be-In," for short) occurred in Golden Gate Park.

Once Chicago had thawed out, on Mother's Day of that year a be-in was held on the North Side in Lincoln Park, followed by a happening on the South Side at Promontory Point. The be-in at Lincoln Park was fairly well covered by the media of the day, but its South Side cousin left barely a trace of evidence behind. But it happened.

And, the whole sunshine-and-daisies hippie counterculture narrative is particularly striking set against the backdrop of Chicago, where just a year earlier Dr. Martin Luther King Jr. marched for open housing. In fact, King stated to reporters in 1966 that

> I've been in many demonstrations all across the South, but I can say that I have never seen—even in Mississippi and Alabama—mobs as hostile and hate-filled as I've seen here in Chicago.[1]

The Human Be-In took place in San Francisco, cast with a whole bunch of lost children and intellectuals. They didn't have the immediate crush of history weighing heavily on them. Those folks had the luxury to just be, flowers in their hair, seemingly untethered to the heaviness of the past.

Chicago's be-ins had a bit more subtext: the ongoing racial tension that exploded the following year (mired in grief), class- and race-based struggles that often manifested themselves in union tussles, and block-by-block skirmishes centered around ongoing neighborhood changes (by the end of the decade, Englewood, on Chicago's South Side, would be nearly 100 percent Black, whereas in the early 1950s it was nearly 100 percent white). And then there was the ever-widening so-called generation gap. Maybe some people were yearning to come together.

The Point, as it is known, was a natural choice for such a be-in. Located in Hyde Park, it has served as a point of convergence for people of all stripes since its opening in 1937, particularly in the form of weddings.

A verdant manmade peninsula jutting off the lakefront, the Point was embroiled in the 2000s in controversy due to the city's proposal to replace its limestone embankment with steel and concrete. Much of the lakefront initially had the limestone treatment, but the stones at most beaches had been removed in the 1990s. A "Save the Point" preservationist movement ensued. Blue "Save the Point" bumper stickers became ubiquitous from the Midway Plaisance to Hyde Park Boulevard. Preservationists prevailed.

I could find only one photo of the 1967 Promontory Point Be-In, published in the July 1967 issue of *Ebony*. A dazzling Black girl with soft black bangs and smile is walking through the shot. She is wearing a suede poncho and sandals while holding a fistful of daisies.

An uncredited photo-editorial accompanies the picture:

> But let's forget it. The dream is over. The Be-ins won't make even a dent in the hate and mistrust and dissension in this country alone. There will still be screams of black and white power, the double-talk of politicians, the fight over open-occupancy, poverty amidst plenty, crime, graft and double dealing. . . . But on second thought, if you do hear that there is going to be a Be-in in your city, go on out to it. Be a human being for at least one afternoon. Some of it might stick.[2]

And so, like a smoke signal, the sentiment of the photo-editorial was sent up to the skies. The response came nearly a year later.

In 1968, Chicago bore America's scar: a seam where two worlds collided in a jagged mess. In the wake of the assassination of Dr. Martin Luther King Jr., people spilled into the streets in protest, in love, in anger, in desperation, in grief.

The city had been simmering for decades, but in 1968 it seethed and boiled. The people cried out for freedom, for hope, for self-determination.

Out of the stew came many things, among them a brave new crop of local cultural affairs television programs aimed at Blacks.

The day after King's assassination, the West Side went up in flames, and more than twenty city blocks were ultimately decimated. The streets were war torn. Mayor Daley imposed a curfew for everyone under the age of twenty-one. More than a few young men commandeered rifles from the Sears on Homan Avenue, broken glass crunching beneath leaning soles. The Loop was essentially shut down, with curfews strictly enforced by police. Downtown businesses were paralyzed with fear of such riotous activity spreading virally downtown (it didn't). Similar curfews were implemented in downtown Chicago in the summer of 2020 (in the wake of the police-involved killing of George Floyd in Minneapolis).

Like much of the country, in 1968 Black Chicago was cloaked in both anger and grief.

Part of the reason that Black Chicagoans felt the assassination of Dr. King so acutely was that he lived in Chicago during 1966 as part of the Chicago Freedom Movement, which activated for open housing. Dr. King's organization, the Southern Christian Leadership Conference (SCLC), had a particularly powerful arm in Chicago known as Operation Breadbasket. During his time in Chicago, King lived on the West Side and organized multiple actions against restrictive housing covenants and other oppressive housing injustices. The demonstrators often met with violent opposition.

In February 1966, *Jet* published an article titled "How King Wages War on Slums in Chicago." He had recently moved into his tiny Hamlin Avenue apartment in Lawndale. It had, according to the article, only a handful of furnishings, and barely enough heat. The writeup declared that, from this threadbare apartment, "King can see the nightmare that was never replaced by his dream." His work in Chicago was setting the groundwork for the Poor Peoples' Campaign: he sought a living minimum wage, to mobilize the unemployed into vocations, and to capture federal funding for rehabilitation of the slums.

Jet noted that the local street gangs were "offering protection to King's staff" and "attending rural 'retreats'" where nonviolence as a technique is explained and urged upon the gangs. Some of that training, which included information on community organizing, resurfaced as the Vice Lords emerged in the late 1960s as the Conservative Vice Lords. But the *Jet* piece made it clear that "such rapport wasn't easy to establish."

James Orange, then a young organizer with the SCLC, bore the scars of that effort. According to the article, some gang members tested his commitment to nonviolence by jumping him a few times. He never fought back. *Jet* related that "he bled with dignity. That broke the ice."

During his stay in Chicago, King went on Wesley South's radio show on WVON, the most powerful Black station in Chicago at the time. Though not Black-owned (at the time it was owned by Leonard and Phil Chess of Chess Records), the station touted a tagline of "Voice of the Negro" and, in addition to music, it offered public affairs and news programming.

On *Wesley South's Hotline*, as the program was called, Dr. King observed that "the demonstrators have not been the violent ones. They have often been the recipients of violence. But, they did not initiate violence."[3]

Although there was some discord among the community regarding his methodology, the general feeling was one of respect for King and his dogged determination.

In April 1968, in the days following the assassination, in a small storefront on Chicago's West Side, Otis Spann (a blues pianist and vocalist) recorded "A Tribute to Martin Luther King." The recording was released on Cry Records, the label was starkly black with block silver print (fig. 1). It was the imprint's only release.

> Yes, fellas . . . I know you had to heard the news
> That happened down in Memphis, Tennessee yesterday?
> There came a sniper
> Wiped Dr. King's life away.[4]

The recording by Otis Spann notes on the label that "profits from this record will be donated to the SCLC."

Out of the rubble of the uprising and borne of fear, a number of Black-focused public affairs shows came to be. The idea was that allowing Blacks a forum to be heard outside of the Black community might retard the growth of another breakdown.

It's hard for two parties to truly come together and express their perspectives when one voice is so much louder than the other, but the resulting efforts were at the very least valiant efforts.

"The rumors were, on the day of Dr. King's funeral, [Blacks] were going to riot," recalled Daddy-O Daylie, who was a disc jockey at WMAQ radio in 1968.[5] He asked Warner Saunders, then executive director of the

FIGURE 1. "A Tribute to Martin Luther King," 45 rpm record. (Photo by the author)

Better Boys Foundation (a popular youth center on the West Side), to be his cohost on a TV program called *For Blacks Only*. The producer was Vernon Jarrett, who was later a columnist at the *Chicago Sun-Times*.

Saunders once stated that, when he started, there were just a few Blacks on the air in Chicago. He taught himself broadcasting by studying tape recordings he made at home.[6]

The public affairs show was initially slated to be a special, but it got such high ratings that local ABC affiliate Channel 7 ran its episodes for eleven years.

Warner Saunders later enjoyed a long career as a local news anchor.

For Blacks Only was part of a fresh trend of programming that provided positive Black roles on television. The trend was so notable that *Ebony* covered the topic in 1969 as "TV Discovers the Black Man." The article heralded the Black faces seen weekly on primetime hits such as *Star Trek*, *Mission Impossible*, and *Peyton Place*. It also spoke of a flood of Black-oriented programming that was created in the wake of riots that had rocked cities across the nation.[7]

Perhaps even more notably, by September 1969 (a scant seven months later), *Ebony* ran a far less glowing article, titled "Black TV: Its Problems and Promises." That piece focused less on glossy dramatic roles and more on Black public-affairs programming airing in Pittsburgh, Detroit, Chicago, and other cities.[8]

"Problems and Promises" dives into the weeds of Black programming, laying out roadblocks that Black producers dealt with, from the pressure to translate for non-Black audiences and the tiny percentage of station budgets allotted for such shows, to the push-and-pull between Black creatives and often-white directors for control.

These issues are still pertinent to makers of Black-targeted programming today; however, back then the issue was compounded because the media landscape was far less fractured. That is, national broadcast television consisted solely of CBS, NBC, and ABC, each providing programming to huge swathes of the public at any given time. Even smaller UHF channels commanded a larger market share in the pre-cable age.

Today, there are many hundreds of channels (plus streaming programming) narrowcasting to highly targeted slices of the pie. But, in 1969, Black Entertainment Television was science fiction; and even before a Black program could be broadcast, it needed to overcome internal hurdles during the production phase.

"Strange things can happen when a script enters the hands of a white director, executive producer, and all white technical crew," the *Ebony* article proclaimed, "Stranger things happen when the white technicians speak in technical vernacular, and the sights and sounds of 'white magic' swirl over the head of a Negro producer for the first time."

In Chicago alone, there was *For Blacks Only*, as well as Jim Tilmon's *Our People* on WTTW, and *A Black's View of the News* on WCIU. The last was an all-Black nightly news program hosted by Don Cornelius and Roy Woods in the years before Don launched *Soul Train* as a local dance and music program in 1970 (also on WCIU).

Television was, in that moment, a flickering medium to express what had been bottled up, to voice what had been silent. And yet, those flashes of Black light were perishable. One lone lost episode of *Our People* survives.[9] No trace of *A Black's View of the News*. Tapes degraded or were destroyed. Erased. Voices rendered mute, again. Yet some city blocks are still seething. And in some cases, particularly on Chicago's West Side, the blocks are still dormant.

From late 2012 until 2017 I produced a Chicago radio show called *The Barber Shop Show* that broadcast live from Carter's Barber Shop in Chicago's Lawndale neighborhood on the West Side. Carter's has been a community anchor for decades. We broadcast on Vocalo, a community-focused urban alternative public radio station. We were also rebroadcast on our sister station, WBEZ (an NPR affiliate).

The show was hosted by veteran broadcaster Richard Steele during my tenure as producer, and we welcomed reporters, activists, musicians, politicians, and other community members for deep-dive conversations on culture and public affairs issue. We focused primarily on issues impacting Chicago's Black and brown communities. Our tiny team was afforded editorial freedom, which allowed us to cover stories that otherwise were not getting media coverage without the internal production hurdles that so many Black media makers face during the story-pitching process.

It wasn't until years later that I considered what we did was a continuation of the mission of that first wave of local Black public-affairs programming.

One 2013 episode of *The Barber Shop Show* featured George Daniels, the charismatic owner of George's Record Room. That popular record store (and community staple) was located for decades on the West Side since George started it in 1969.

Though George's was a small store in a field populated at the time by huge chains like Sam Goody, George was very influential in the music industry. He at one time "organized close to twenty thousand Black record stores across the country" to combat what he saw as injustices toward small Black retailers in the music industry.[10]

George shared with us that "the [distributors] would come to the record store and do displays, you know, like your windows and your walls?" He was talking about record label promotional pieces, like a full-size cardboard cutout of Chaka Khan, or an SOS Band poster.

We would thank them! I was so happy, you know, to get some new stuff. Didn't know they were supposed to pay us. That was revenue space within our store. That was advertising. So as time had gone on, I joined the white trade organization, which is NARM, National Association of Recording Merchandisers. These were the big chains, the Sam Goodys and the Tower Records, and so and so forth. And my fellow [small] retailers were like "Man, that's too big for you! They got you know, they got two and three . . . five hundred stores," [to which he replied,] "Well they started with one."

And so, I went in there and all the things they talked about, I scaled it down to one. And so, I befriended some and they would tell me what they were getting [from distributors]. I said, "get out of here!" So, I put together a little marketing packet for the next meeting me and my fellow Black retailers had with one of the major distributors.

I walk in there, and we sit around talking. And I tell the senior VP, "Here's something for you to look at." He said, "What's that?" I said, "Eh. Just something." So, he looked over it. . . . Eyes popped open. He left the room. He went and told everybody, I guess, the staff. And he came back and pulled me out.

[The senior VP] said, "George, well, you know, we don't pay for advertising in stores." I said, "You wanna rephrase that? Do you know I'm a member of NARM, now?" And so, they made adjustments, and they said, "Okay, George, you know, we'll take care of you; but, just don't say much." Man, I was like Gabriel, I was blowin' in horns all across America, and I started getting [small Black music retailers] paid.

George wasn't committed just to his fellow Black businessmen, though. On the community level, he organized back-to-school events and toy drives through the store.

Around the time of this visit to *The Barber Shop Show*, George's Music Room was shuttered (his focus was on a satellite location at Midway Airport), but he still owned the property where the West Side George's Music Room stood. George was invested in the neighborhood, and his intention was to reopen the original store. That is until one incident broke his heart: vandals broke in and, in short order, destroyed what he had built over decades. Reporter Robin Robinson interviewed Daniels for a television news piece that aired footage of the wreckage. This wasn't simply a break-in with some overturned chairs and broken glass, but absolutely gruesome. It looked as though someone had delighted in wreaking utter destruction.

> It hurt because didn't nobody come from outside the community to do that. They was some people within the area. For all the things you assume that you did: you hired the children, and you helped feed many families. . . . I mean, I had sports figures come during Thanksgiving . . . everybody benefitted.

He noted the close-knit nature of his customer base.

Richard asked George if anyone had reached out to help him rebuild. George replied, "A number of people are really apologetic. It's really discouraging. I wanted to create a development . . . [in] that block. Like the guy in Harlem [Geoffrey Canada, founder of the Harlem Children's Zone], if he can make a difference, one block at a time . . ."

Always a community-minded entrepreneur in the tradition of Black Chicago's best and brightest, he felt particularly wounded that this affront came from his own beloved community.

George lamented:

> We're so depressed over here, when the economy slipped and fell, if you will. . . . We're the ones that are suffering behind it. When you look at our areas, it's like a desert. We have to remember, in 1969 when I opened, it was the year after the riots of Dr. King. And there are still vacant lots in our community that are still sitting vacant since 1968! Let's go fast-forward. When Rodney King riots in LA [happened in 1992], just as much damage. But you can't even tell. It's all been repaired. . . . Lawndale, the West Side community has still been paying for the riots of 1968.

The West Side location of George's Music Room has yet to reopen.

Gus Rickette, founder of Uncle Remus Chicken, another West Side staple, was also featured on that episode of *The Barber Shop Show*, along with his daughter, Charmaine Alfred, who runs the business today.

The youngest of twelve children, she shared that she was "not really expected to work in the business."

> We had been on the West Side for fifty years. That's our roots. Our foundation. But my vision was to just expand the brand and create a system where we could just grow. . . . There are so many proud moments I have from taking on the legacy of my parents starting this business. You know, [in 2014 Uncle

21

Remus Chicken celebrated] our fiftieth year. I am most proud that all of our hires are from the community. . . . We believe in second chances. . . . I have a joke: "Ex is a prerequisite to work for us," you know? [*Chuckles.*] "You're an ex-con, you're an ex-addict, you're an ex-something. . . . I often try to instill leadership in them.

I have an employee that was homeless about a year or so ago. He came to volunteer, to help me clean up one of the stores when we were opening in [West suburban] Broadview. . . . And I told him we were going to work his way into a job. And he's now my assistant manager.

She reiterated for emphasis: "He was homeless a year and a half ago."

Her father, Gus Rickette, talked about his deep commitment to the community that supported Uncle Remus Chicken all these years.

During the radio show, host Richard Steele mentioned that businesses that take in a lot of cash (like a chicken shack) are at risk for a stick-up. He asked Gus if they'd ever been robbed in their many years in business. Gus replied with the following story:

We was very liberal for us feeding peoples. This particular night it was very, very cold. And there wasn't that many peoples on the streets. And so, this man came to the door, and the door was locked. We was in the back. . . . He knocked on the door. . . . I was sittin' back at the counter having a cup of coffee. So, I went and opened the door and let him in. And said "Have a cup of coffee." He says, "Yes. It's cold out here."

And so, having a cup of coffee, he began to talk to me. And he said he had spent eleven years in penitentiary. And he came out to stick me up. We sit there till daylight, drinking coffee, and he had two . . . two guns. When he left, he left one with me. 'Bout three, four months [later] he came back and got it. Took the other one with him.

Call it what you will: cultural currency, respect, kismet for kindness, whatever you believe saved Gus from what could have been a violent (and pointedly desperate) incident, love for Black people from Black people prevailed that day.

The Rickettes have been in business at that same West Madison location over forty years. At the time of that near-miss, they'd been there about fifteen. And though Uncle Remus opened their first South Side location in 2015, according to Gus, their commitment to the West Side has never wavered.

The thing that makes Black Chicago special is present in a particularly high concentration on the West Side. Maybe that's because of the pattern of migration in Chicago.

The first wave of the Great Migration of Black people from the Deep South to Chicago filled in what became known as the Low End or the Black Bottom: a slim band of the South Side in the early decades of the twentieth century. The West Side didn't really start becoming an area with a Black majority until the 1950s. That wave (composed of primarily Mississippians) to Chicago's Lawndale, Douglas Park, Garfield Park, and Austin areas flowed on until the 1970s, long after the migration had slowed to a trickle to the South Side.

So, in a sense, the migrant's hustle, as well as a certain southern sensibility and flow, are fresher and more uncut on the West Side than in other parts of Chicago. To put it another way, the cultural juice is from tree-ripened fruit. Some blocks even formed Mississippi hometown associations because such a high concentration of folks hailed from the likes of Sunflower or Grenada.

But the West Side is remarkably absent from many discussions of Chicago, both internally and externally. The term "South Side" becomes shorthand for Black. And, even within the hierarchy of Black Chicago, there is an ongoing rift between West Siders and South Siders. Depending on the vantage point, one side or the other never quite measures up.

To be fair, all over Chicago (regardless of race) there is a tribal aspect, folks trying to get a handle on you are prone to ask what high school you went to, or perhaps what Catholic parish you are from. But, between the South and West Sides in particular, there is a strange Othering that happens that I consider soul-dampening. There is a rift built around time-honored negative regional stereotypes that all too often keep the South and West Sides socially separated.

I think that rift holds us all back. The Pan-African movement began because Black people realized their energy was best spent by utilizing their power and resources collectively rather than separately. Ghana *and* Haiti are stronger together than Ghana *or* Haiti alone.

That's why I use the term "Black Chicago," particularly for the purposes of this book. It is inclusive of both the West Side and the South Side.

The West Side is a glorious boxer that is still fighting, scuffed gloves on guard. Still bearing the scars of 1968 on its brow. Knocked down by factory divestment in the third and fifth rounds. Still pushing, still hustling. Neighborhoods are still vital with energy. With promise. And with buy-in from community members and from stakeholders like the Better Boys Foundation.

The Better Boys Foundation (now BBF Family Services) was started in 1961 on the West Side as a gym with a youth boxing program to keep kids off the street.

When one of the youths from the gym died tragically, the founder, Joe Kellman, realized that boxing was "the lure and not the cure," so the program began to offer social services as well.[11]

In the mid-1970s, the Better Boys Foundation staged *The Black Fairy*, a then-popular play by local author Useni Eugene Perkins, through its LaMont Zeno Community Theater program. The play was directed by Pemon Rami, a cultural worker who has served as a mentor to many, including actor and director Robert Townsend. I talked to Townsend on *Reclaimed Soul* in the summer of 2018.

> [Pemon Rami] and his wife, Maséqua Myers, they were kind of my first role models because they introduced me to theater at sixteen years old and I was on the West Side doing theater, at LaMont Zeno, and I was on the South Side at X-BAG, Experimental Black Actors Guild. But, Mr. Rami was the one who got me into show business, really, because I was an extra in *Mahogany* [1975] because he was the casting director and he got us involved. And then, he told the casting director for *Cooley High* [1976], which was my first speaking part, that they should see me. And so, I'm forever indebted to him because he was the one who allowed me to really see what show business was about and taste it firsthand.[12]

The LaMont Zeno Foundation released a cast LP of *The Black Fairy* in very limited numbers that nonetheless testifies to the power of the story, the music, and the cast's performances. This was not a low-budget recording. It was recorded at Paul Serrano's PS Studios, where Deniece Williams and Earth, Wind & Fire also recorded and which were located near what is now a McCormick Place annex on Chicago's near South Side. There are two iterations of the album cover, one is by AfriCOBRA artist Barbara Jones-Hogu (the other is by Akosua Bandele).

AfriCOBRA (African Commune of Bad Relevant Artists) was a group of artists founded by Jones-Hogu, Gerald Williams, Jeff Donaldson, Wadsworth Jerrell, and Jae Jerrell.[13] They were committed to positive expressions of Black people and culture. Jones-Hogu had a long history in the Black Arts Movement in Chicago as an artist and as a community organizer. Years earlier, Jones-Hogu contributed to the iconic *Wall of Respect* mural at 43rd Street and Langley Avenue that was created in 1967 through the Organization of Black American Culture (OBAC) collective.

Because *The Black Fairy* has not been performed in many years, and there is no publicly available typescript, I referred to my LP for the following synopsis.[14] It is not lost on me that I've translated an LP into text that is itself a translation of a play. In each translation, a sense was lost: first sight, then sound.

The play opens to find the Black Fairy (played by Patricia Crawford) lamenting that she has no magic "like the white fairies" to "make every black child free."

She meets Johnny (Vincent Hardman), a young Black boy who apparently has been jaded by city life and doesn't believe in much of anything. He tells her that "nobody cares about black people" because if they did he and his family "wouldn't have to eat beans and cornbread every day." He tells her that Black people have nothing to be proud of. He exclaims "you can't make me happy. You're black. Just like me." What the Black Fairy discovers, however, is that her magic lies in the truth.

The Blackbird (Denise Llorens) tells the Black Fairy that the "magic of truth is much more powerful than the magic of make believe." The Blackbird tells her to tell the children that they are beautiful and Black. The blackbird sings sweetly:

Tell them that being Black is nothing to be ashamed of
Tell them that being Black is something to be proud of
Tell them they are beautiful
As beautiful as the stars

The Black Fairy is taken on the wings of the Blackbird back in time, to learn about her heritage from the Queen Mother (Masequa Myers), so that she will be able to share her knowledge with the children.

As a teenager, Robert Townsend was a part of the original production of *The Black Fairy*. He shared with me: "I played Stagger Lee in *The Black Fairy*, and I played the Signifying Monkey and Mr. Moon. I played four characters, but that's where I learned." He missed the recording dates for the LP because he was in school.

Townsend went on to direct and star in major motion pictures like *The Five Heartbeats*, *Meteor Man*, and his breakthrough film, *Hollywood Shuffle*. But his love of the performing arts started on the West Side of Chicago. "It was important for me to see people of color writing, directing, producing and acting, and that was always in my bloodstream because I saw it firsthand."

The Black Fairy recording features blues-infused soulful jazz by Tony Llorens and Jami Ayinde, with powerful horns by Earl "Chico" Freeman. Chico, the son of the legendary Chicago horn player Von Freeman, is a member of the storied Association for the Advancement of Creative Musicians (AACM). Chico also played with blues musicians like Memphis Slim while still living in Chicago.[15]

In one song from the play, called "Afrikan Children," drenched in keyboards and street-corner doo-wop harmonies, Denise Llorens sings,

> We are black like the starless night
> We're all children of Afrika
> We are ebony like burnt toast
> We're all children of Afrika
> We are brown like peanut butter
> We are chocolate like the candy bar
> Amber like sweet, sweet honey . . .

In the end, the Black Fairy comes to understand that her magic is in herself. It is in her "total being." A lineage that stretches from Egypt and West Africa to the plantation, and to Harlem. With no magical make-believe.

In the finale, the cast sings, "Hey Black child, do you know who you are? / Do you know you can do what you want to do? / And tomorrow your nation will be what you want it to be."

Listening to my original LP, which is over forty years old, it struck me what it must have been like to be a little one watching this performed on the stage. It also strikes me that it is nothing short of a miracle that this testament made its way to me. Most of these community plays have scant documentation. This one lives. It shimmers and shines. It sings with a message of hope and pride that is baked into Black Chicago, a message that we need now as much as ever before.

Ending my conversation with Robert Townsend, I mentioned his long running sitcom, *The Parent 'Hood*, a 1990s program that featured a Black family that I used to watch religiously growing up. The daughter (played by Reagan Gomez-Preston) was about my age, and Black shows with strong loving families were in the minority at the time.

I told Townsend, half stuttering with sincerity, "I was in high school around that time, and I just thought that was a really great program. Thank you for that. I just wanna say thank you."

He replied: "Well, you know I created that show for you because the thing about it is, I wanted the show to be entertaining, but I also put my little messages in there, so that, you can kind of look at your life and say, 'I can identify with this and I can have a good time,' and it's silly, but it's also, 'there's some messages you can take home.' So, thank you."

FOUND

GROOVES GHOSTLY WHITE

Years ago, I found a lovely promotional 45 rpm record—Curtis Mayfield's "We Got to Have Peace" (fig. 2). Grooves ghostly white. The single is taken from Mayfield's *Roots* album, released in 1971. *Roots* was released months before the *Superfly* soundtrack, and it is just as wonderful. Released on Chicago's Curtom Records, the rare promotional record was crafted of creamy white wax. Colored vinyl from this period, 45s in particular, is quite rare. Colored vinyl records were generally created to make people (DJs in particular) stop and take notice; even some forty years later, notice I did.

In the year following the epic 1970 album *Curtis*, Mayfield mounted a campaign to fully express himself as a solo artist in ways he could not as a member of the soul group the Impressions. As early as the mid-sixties, some of the Impressions' most beloved songs (including "Keep on Pushing" [1964] and "People Get Ready" [1965]) were implicitly political, intended to inspire listeners. "I had the love thing very strong," Mayfield recalled in 1975:

> We had songs like "Keep on Pushing," and "Amen." Even "It's All Right" was a song of inspiration to me. You know:
>
> > When you wake up early in the morning

FIGURE 2. "We Got to Have Peace," 45 rpm record. (Photo by the author)

> Feeling sad like many of us do
> Hum a little Soul
> Make life your goal
> And surely something's got to come to you.[1]

Mayfield further reflected:

I think a lot of that came from my grandmother [a minister at the Traveling Soul Spiritualist Church], and I guess even as I slept through many sermons they kind of piled up in my head. That was where "Keep on Pushing" and "Choice of Colors" came from. Every once in a while, I felt it was important to say something more than just "shake your shaggy shaggy" or "do wow," you know?

According to poet and soul singer avery r. young, the ministry inherent in Mayfield's music was no accident. To the contrary, Chicago soul music hash gospel music DNA coded deep within its bone marrow. young argues that Black Chicago's topology produces a unique mix of gospel and soul, the sacred and the profane:

> Chicago Soul music is . . . merging of two gifts that Chicago has given the world: the Blues and the Gospel. And what happens in most spaces, particularly the South, you have the church that's by itself and then you have the juke joint . . . usually in separate spaces in a town or a city. But, in Chicago on a given street, the tavern and the church house are next-door neighbors.
>
> And what happens, when anybody passes there, right at the gangway [or alley], there's usually a bleed of what's coming from the church house and what's coming from the tavern. And that is the crux of soul music.
>
> There's one thing where the preacher is saving souls, and I believe Pops Staples and Mavis [Staples] was specifically about saving humanity. Encouraging folks to be humane to each other. Which is a very different ministry. Not watered down, but a very different ministry.
>
> Curtis Mayfield, what he wanted to do with that bleed, he wanted to make it real pretty. I don't think Baba Curtis ever wrote on a sheet of paper. He wrote on the sky.[2]

Mayfield frequently worked heavenly themes into his music. In "People Get Ready," Mayfield announced that all manner of freedom was near, riding the metaphorical train commonly found in Black spirituals such as "The Gospel Train." He understood that "the Train is somewhat of a symbol of God Himself coming to take on and bring all the people who have somewhat gotten themselves together and may possibly be able to venture over to the other side of the world . . . or heaven."[3]

But, despite the passage of the Civil Rights Act of 1964, the same social struggles (such as poverty, injustice, and blight) were omnipresent in the Black community through the end of the decade. Mayfield wanted to share messages of uplift that were more insistent and urgent, and he needed more than a metaphor to get his messages across. One of his first political records was "We're a Winner," recorded at RCA's Chicago studios in 1967 (studios Mayfield later bought). The session included a lively audience that added encouraging whoops and hollers to the recording. Before the song fully lifts off, a woman distinctly calls out "sock it to me, baby!" in the lull between horn stabs. These lines—

I don't mind leaving here
to show the world we have no fear
Cause we're a winner
and everybody knows the truth
We'll just keep on pushin'
Like your leaders tell you to.[4]

—allude to a more pointed, assertive stance. Yet the lyrics still maintained some sense of conservatism, suggesting that listeners acquiesce to leaders.

Mayfield had long been interested in the business side of recording, stating in 1975 that he had "always respected [Black-owned Chicago record label] Vee Jay and all the independent companies . . . especially Motown and their ability to do great things in the business."[5] In 1968, after years of recording for ABC-Paramount and writing and producing for other artists on a variety of labels (Okeh and Constellation among them), Mayfield put his money where his mouth was and opened his own label at 8141 South Stony Island Avenue in partnership with his then-manager, Eddie Thomas. Curtom Records was in fact his fourth foray into independent labels; Mayfield Records, Thomas Records, and Windy C Records all came before, but his Curtom label had much higher stakes. While his earlier labels produced other performers (most successful of which being the Five Stairsteps), the lion's share of Curtom's production centered on his compositions. It would then become the home of his group, the Impressions. Armed with a freshly inked distribution deal from Neil Bogart at Buddah Records, he was gambling with the Impressions' ten-year track record of success, leaving ABC-Paramount (a major label) to chart his own path to industry success.

"This Is My Country" (1968) was one of Curtom Records' first releases. The song's political message was even more pointed than "We're a Winner," with lines like these:

I've paid three hundred years or more
Of slave driving, sweat, and welts on my back
This is my country
Too many have died in protecting my pride
For me to go second class
We've survived a hard blow and I want you to know
That you must face us at last.[6]

The phrase "This is my country" is still loaded for a multitude of reasons fifty years after the Impressions laid it down on wax. African Americans, a population with a long, multigenerational lineage in the United States, are a unique tribe: we are in many ways alienated from other non-Black Americans (as evidenced in "This Is My Country"). A couple of radio stations banned the song in late 1968; some disc jockeys and radio executives considered the song too radical. In response to that idea, Todd Mayfield (son to Curtis) posed to me the following question: "What is radical? One person's radical is another person's revolutionary. It just depends on what side of the line you're on."[7]

In April 2018, fifty years after Martin Luther King Jr. was assassinated on that balcony at the Lorraine Motel, and nearly fifty years after the release of "This Is My Country," I discussed the idea of "just Blackness" with Naomi Beckwith. Naomi's star rose as an Associate Curator at the Studio Museum In Harlem, but, at the time, she was Manilow Senior Curator at the Museum of Contemporary Art in Chicago. Naomi curated 2015's *The Freedom Principle: Experiments in Art and Music, 1965 to Now*, a multimedia exhibition built around the legacy of Chicago's AACM, and in 2018 she co-curated a gorgeous survey of the work of Howardena Pindell, among other brilliant shows. She is also a Black Chicagoan, raised in Hyde Park.

AYANA CONTRERAS: We were talking about this idea of "just Black" not being valued in the same way [as Black people with backgrounds directly connected to countries outside the United States].

NAOMI BECKWITH: Well, exactly. You know, I've been in communities where people always ask about international origin. Where you came from.

AC: They want you to be Jamaican, or something?

NB: Jamaican, Dominican, Haitian. Trinidadian is a big one [*laughs*]. And, you know, all that's wonderful and fine. One should really find some pride in one's national origins. Chicago is not an immigrant community in that way.

Not to say that it doesn't have people of Black descent or African descent who are immigrants, but its sense of belongingness is about belonging to this community in the U.S. We are not ex-pats. We are not from elsewhere. We are not trying to make distinctions between ourselves and other folks who look like us and even those who do not. [We are] trying to be together.

People often would ask when I was in New York, "Where are you from?" And I would say "Chicago." And then they would ask, "But, where are your parents from?" And I would say, "Chicago." And then, they would say, "Bu-Bu-But, your grandparents?!"

There was a sense that one could not be a Black person in the US and . . . have a long heritage in this country. And my upbringing in Chicago taught me this place is mine, and that I have to claim that.

Because that question of "Where are you from?" isn't just about "What kind of special Black are you? What do you want to brag about that isn't about being a basic American Negro?," which has its own class implications. But it is also about not feeling like you belong here. And some people take that as a romantic notion, but to me that's not cute. You really need to be effective where you are.[8]

Back in the 1960s, the message of "This Is My Country" resonated with its target audiences and it was a hit on Black radio. However, Fred Cash and Sam Gooden (the other members of the Impressions) were becoming more and more uncomfortable with Mayfield's increasingly edgy material. Though he continued to write and produce material for the Impressions, Mayfield began his solo career in 1970, which allowed him to voice his most personal and dogmatic ideas without having to deal with group politics; his first solo single was "(Don't Worry) If There's Hell Below, We're All Going to Go."

An apocalyptic Afro-Latin-tinged funk romp, the recording was his boldest message to date. In his initial solo outings, Mayfield's songs were

FOUND

markedly longer, the basslines were funkier, African percussion became prominent, and the horns were a bit jauntier. Albums were bound together with loose themes. Though he had acquired great mastery of the three-minute radio-ready single track, Mayfield enjoyed using the album format to more fully express his artistic vision. Commenting on record industry conventions in the sixties, he noted in 1975 that "usually you put all your B sides on an album, along with the single records you had put out. Very few people ever thought of recording an album as a complete concept, a story to tell from the first cut to the last to a point that even if you just read the titles of the songs they would just about make up their own paragraph."[9]

Mayfield exhibited an unwavering commitment to exploring the full spectrum of Black experiences through his songs and their political messaging. Mayfield was particularly keen to express the voices of urban Black men: those who struggled, scratched, loved, dreamed, and believed. Despite this focus, he wrote nuanced compositions from women's perspectives, as well (for instance, cuts from the soundtracks to *Claudine* [1974] and *Sparkle* [1976]). His political soul sound is still relevant today, wrought with an eloquent and earthy simplicity. "Move on Up" is a Black cultural anthem. "We Got to Have Peace," the soul composition etched into my ghost-white vinyl record, presents a bassline so much larger than life it might be misclassified as menacing save for the jubilant message holding the center:

> And the people in our neighborhood
> They would if they only could
> Meet and shake the other's hand
> Work together for the good of the land[10]

What happens, though, when a cultural artifact is no longer revered? Initially, I counted it a privilege to hold that ghost-white vinyl. To bear witness to an artifact; a moment in time, captured and etched. One day years later I proudly showed my creamy-white 45 rpm record to Todd Mayfield. He quipped that, as children, he and his siblings used to use copies of the record (not a chart-topping success by any means) as Frisbees.

* * *

St. Laurence's, a Roman Catholic church on Chicago's South Side, finally came down in 2014. The grounds, which also included a rectory and a school, had already deteriorated from a devastating fire and years of

FIGURE 3. The parishioner, 2014. (Photo by the author)

wanton neglect. It was no longer a sanctuary; the Archdiocese of Chicago closed the church a decade ago.[11] On a honeyed Sunday evening during St. Laurence's last days, a former parishioner dressed in a dove-gray suit came to pay his respects (fig. 3). He had attended St. Laurence's school next door as a child. We stood speechless for a long time. I did not ask his name. It was hard to express the stunning beauty of this building, even as it crumbled before our eyes.

According to Preservation Chicago, the buildings dated back to 1911. The complex was listed as one of Chicago's seven most threatened buildings by Preservation Chicago in 2011, the year of the buildings' one hundredth birthday.[12] Landmarks Illinois, a similar organization dedicated to historic preservation, stated that "this collection of buildings is one of Chicago's most intact and impressive early twentieth-century religious complexes."[13] And yet, it was being demolished, disassembled brick by brick. Mortar was knocked off as if part of a requiem ritual: *clink-clink-cla-clink, clink-clink-cla-clink*. Dislodged bricks were stacked gingerly on wood pallets as though they were the sacrament.

Those holy gold bricks were also collected by salvagers. That same day, a salvage worker told me that "some people are coming to get the bricks and whatnot, saying they want to save them, for memories."[14] Somewhere in the midst of this rubble lay a metaphor. Was St. Laurence's a sleeping giant, or a fallen warrior? Watching the building's slow decay as plant matter took parishioners' places inside the sanctuary had been surreal; now it had been quickened.

One summer, I taught a radio production program for teenagers in Bronzeville. I had a student who was terribly shy, shut tight like a pistachio most days. I once asked her to sum up the toll an abandoned building takes on a block and the community as a whole. Her words still haunt me: "They are a black hole."

Of course. Everything dark circulates around abandoned buildings: drugs, crime, strife. Darkness itself is housed within it. Yet, knowing the potential for such darkness within, St. Laurence's still shone bright especially on sunny, cloudless days. A passerby might almost forget that time was ravaging the building from the inside out. If a building could be proud despite ruin, this building was just that. Artist and community resident Theaster Gates told me he had looked into saving it while the building still stood, but it was beyond repair by then. Even to a man known for resurrecting lifeless buildings, St. Laurence's days were numbered. I cannot help but feel as though had this building been built on the North Side and not in Grand Crossing, its fate might have been different. Its propensity for love might have been its saving grace. Its role as anchor, its identity as connective tissue, might have been sufficient to earn it clemency. The faceless remnants of rubble maintained until its final moments the power to stop pedestrians in their tracks. To me, this adoration and devotion begs the question: can holiness ever be removed from a communally sanctified space?

* * *

Neat rows of distinctive bungalows line the streets in a collection of South Side neighborhoods known together as the Bungalow Belt. Many of these homes predate the Great Depression, but they have lately suffered a disturbing fate. As longtime owners of these homes age and pass away, later generations have been selling or losing their family homes at an alarming rate. This trend began roughly in the 1990s, persisted through the economic crisis of 2008, and continues today, creating a perfect storm of community erosion.[15] Once proudly manicured blocks are now marred by boarded-up windows and overgrown shrubbery. The homes that families worked for a generation to own are being lost in the span of a year or two. Some are sold or foreclosed on due to the monetary strains created by owning an aging home; others are neglected and even given away because younger generations do not value urban home ownership or the legacy of their family homes.

Erased is a narrative that author Mary Pattillo documents in her 1999 *Black Picket Fences: Privilege and Peril among the Black Middle Class*. She describes how the "black middle class and their residential enclaves are nearly invisible to the nonblack public because of the intense (and mostly negative) attention given to poor urban ghettos."[16] Due to the geographic proximity of urban middle- and working-class Black neighborhoods, their survival is inextricably linked. Members of the Black middle class are by no means rich; many are hard-working, blue-collar people. At the same time, urban geography means their access to disposable income positively impacts all the communities around them. Nevertheless, a more mobile generation has left their family homes and communities behind for a multitude of reasons. What becomes of the institutions and buildings rendered simple memories in this generation's absent neglect?

In April 2017, *Crain's Chicago Business* real estate journalist Dennis Rodkin heralded the advent of "the rebuilders of Chicago's Southland" in a cover story.

A small set of urban pioneers is buying property on the south side and in the south suburbs, not with gentrification or house-flipping—let alone price appreciation—in mind. Rather, they're staking a claim, hoping to recapture something that has been lost: a community that may not be prosperous now but could be again if more people were to follow their lead.[17]

The article profiles people who bought the homes they grew up in, and others just trying to set down roots for their own kids. The scale of these "rebuilders" is small, but notable. There is a ripening belief in resurrecting these once-loved homes. The stakes are high.

Meanwhile, the resolution of St. Laurence's story was bittersweet. Though the church and rectory did not survive, St. Laurence's School across the street was spared. There are plans for it to be reborn as an arts center in a project spearheaded by Theaster Gates. Meanwhile, the plot where the church and rectory stood was redeveloped as an assisted-living facility. Unfortunately, such an ending is not that common in communities like Grand Crossing, which has multiple railroad tracks running through it but little in terms of developments and commerce.

Society has been infected by Hollywood's idea of the narrative arc, the idea that conflict always leads to a neat, happy ending. That polite termination is as false as sixties-era dental caps. What we get in real life, right here in Grand Crossing, is a bumper crop of disappointments, augmented by the occasional rags-to-riches tale that becomes more believable by its common proximity. If only one of us had made it, the story could be written off as an anomaly, but in aggregate those occasional stories become just enough to hang our hopes on. The corner that cradled St. Laurence's for a century began to be redeveloped within a few years of the church's demolition. That story should not be seen as an anomaly; rather, it is just one element of an intricately linked pattern of overcoming that maps Black Chicago. Those stories are our community birthright.

STAX FAX

BLACK CHRISTMAS BEGAT A
BLACK LOVE PROCESSION

Often, used-record stores smell like rotting flowers: It is the smell of de-
caying cardboard, a smell I improbably often long for.

The week of Christmas 2008, I was in Memphis, Tennessee. A half-
hearted chill hung languidly in the air.

Behind the register at Shangri-La Records, coddled in a cellophane sleeve,
sat a vintage copy of *Stax Fax* (fig. 4).[1] Covering the lean magazine was an
image of a young Black boy alongside an older Black gentleman who points
to something far in the distance on which their eyes are trained. Apart from
the words *Stax Fax*, bold black against shocking pink, and the date—December 1969—there were no hints as to the contents inside. Without even
slipping it out of its sleeve, I plunked down $100 for the magazine. That was
a considerable sum for me. But, I love Stax Records. In December 1969, the
Memphis-based label was on the brink of a revolution, of a *soul explosion*.
By that year, the label had discovered that it had inadvertently signed away
its back catalog in a distribution deal with Atlantic Records. That included
work by its biggest star, Otis Redding, who had died in a plane crash only two
years earlier. The label was in the midst of recording around twenty different
albums simultaneously in order to build a new catalog. Although Stax was
once a conservative singles-minded label with its acts (like Booker T. and

FIGURE 4. Front cover of *Stax Fax*, December 1969. (Author's personal collection)

the MGs) clad in matching sharkskin suits, changing times dictated that it let its artists' hair (and their tracks) grow longer. One of Stax-subsidiary Enterprise's new albums was Isaac Hayes's *Hot Buttered Soul*. The second track on the first side, "Walk On By," clocked in at twelve minutes of psychedelic, symphonic, soulful glory. Knowing that backstory made the slim 1969 issue of *Stax Fax* all the more appealing to me.

A few days later, I tore open the cellophane sleeve swaddling the magazine. Only then did I realize that this particular issue of *Stax Fax*, a fan and industry publication with very low circulation, was in fact dedicated to Chicago and not Memphis. Inside, articles detailed Chicago cultural news, such as Operation Breadbasket and Chicago's first Black Expo. A jolt of electricity ran through my body. That this magazine would wind up in a young Chicagoan's hands after it had, perhaps, spent nearly forty years in Memphis, Tennessee, felt like kismet—I was astounded.

Where did the story detailed within this magazine begin?

First, let's go back to September 2015, to 45th Street and King Drive, next door to the Parkway Ballroom, in front of the Chicago Defender building. A group of Black artists in front of the building, convened by fellow artist-filmmaker Cauleen Smith, embarked on what Smith called a Black Love Procession. The parade featured an ice cream truck, balloons, and banners. Some marchers handed out flowers. A soundtrack of empowering vintage Chicago soul I had curated for the event filled the air. I was bringing up the rear of the procession, trailing behind on purple-and-white roller skates. According to a 2015 Hyperallergic article about the event,

> On the banners carried by marchers, [Cauleen] Smith had emblazoned quotes from a famous Bronzeville citizen, the great poet Gwendolyn Brooks. Quotes were taken from Brooks's poem "The Second Sermon on the Warpland," and included phrases and words such as "Conduct Your Blooming," "Noise," and, "Whirlwind," sparkling high above the procession.
>
> "This poem ['The Second Sermon on the Warpland'] is a love letter to working class black people," Smith said. "Before I ever set eyes on Chicago or Bronzeville I loved this poem. I believe that I live in Bronzeville now because of Ms. Brooks' luminous and rigorous poetry. She wrote that poem and ended it with her wish and her will for us: 'Conduct Your Blooming In the Noise and the Whip of the Whirlwind.' What more could one want for the people she loves?"[2]

Smith was spiritually led by our poetic ancestor. That day, we were spiritually fed by the sonic energy of our melodic ancestors. My home-grown mixtape included tracks by the Pharaohs, Original Breed, Opportunity Please Knock Chorus, and Curtis Mayfield. As it blared from a beige trailing rick, the songs amplified the sentiment of love and empowerment through identity. This message resonated with and deeply reverberated through the artists and their communities, then and now; songs had titles such as "All This Talk about Freedom" and "I Am Somebody."

"I am somebody," a catchphrase popularized by the Reverend Jesse Jackson, caught fire in the streets in 1968. The year before, the collaborative *Wall of Respect* had been erected in Bronzeville, the most well-known of many such culture-affirming murals that popped up across Black Chicago by artists such as Mitchell Caton (best known for "Rip Off/Universal [Jazz] Alley" at South 50th St. and St. Lawrence Ave.). The phrase "I am somebody" demanded recognition of those who rallied around it. It demanded respect. The poem from which the phrase comes, written by Georgia activist the Reverend William H. Borders, exclaims

I am
God's child
I am
Somebody.[3]

Reverend Jackson used "I Am Somebody" during his youth activism. At the start of the 1970s, he and the children of *Sesame Street* recited the poem together during his 1971 appearance on that show, bringing Borders's words to mainstream America. Jackson would again spotlight the poem the following year when he performed it at the 1972 Wattstax Summer Festival at the Los Angeles Coliseum. Slightly predating Jackson's public performances, this energy of self-respect and self-love drove musicians to commit the phrase "I am somebody" to wax.

In 1968, a Chicago Soul group called the Original Breed released a single titled "I Am Somebody" on the tiny Karol label. A member of the group, Wayne Readus, wrote the song, including these lines: "But came the day I found myself. And now I know just who I am. / I am somebody, yes somebody."[4] In a 2006 interview with Bob Abrahamian of WHPK Radio, Readus explained that the song reflected the "atmosphere of the day. [Original Breed was] trying to find something that would touch people."[5] In 1969, WVON music director Richard Pegue adapted the poem for a single he produced for Toddlin Town Records, "I Am Somebody," by the Brothers and Sisters. The group consisted of Claude Wyatt, Billy Smith, Pat James, and Margaret Norfleet. They exclaimed in interwoven harmonies: "I may be young, / But I am / Somebody!"[6]

I intentionally chose the song, digitized from the original 45 rpm single, to form an essential part of the Black Love Procession's sonic landscape. The small band of artists parading down King Drive represented a moment when the past collided joyfully with the future. Calls for unity, community love, and cultural renewal were ringing down the same streets as they had forty-five years earlier during another unique event connected to the Reverend Jesse Jackson.

Black Christmas was organized in 1968 in Chicago by Operation Breadbasket, a SCLC-extension led by Jackson from 1967 to 1971. An article in my newly acquired December 1969 issue of *Stax Fax*, edited by famed Stax Records singer-songwriter and publicist Deanie Parker, laid out the specifics of the event. According to *Stax Fax*, Black Christmas "involves the development of black consciousness through new imagery, which expresses the reality that 'I Am Somebody' and 'We Are Somebody.'" The event reimagined myriad Christmas imagery from a Black perspective; Black Santa, for example, came "from the South Pole by way of the Equator and his attire is a black velvet dashiki trimmed with the colors of the Ghana flag, red, green and yellow."[7] However, Black Santa was not the only significant cultural contribution to come out of Black Christmas.

Beginning in the late 1960s, singer-songwriter Sidney Barnes recorded with the Rotary Connection at Chess Records. Iconic singer Donny Hathaway was on the scene during that time, and as Barnes remembers, Donny would come and hang out at his lakefront apartment on Rush Street:

> Donny Hathaway used to do my lead sheets for ten dollars a piece. He wasn't singing—he was just playing the piano around Chess. So, I thought he was a great talent! I said, "Donny, you gotta sing." He said, "They don't want me to sing, I can't sing."[8]

Donny's earliest recordings betray that he initially sang with a lisp.

Though Hathaway signed on as a solo artist with Atlantic in 1969, he was still prolifically working on arrangements and songwriting for others as a producer and arranger at Curtis Mayfield's Curtom Records. From 1968 to 1970, Hathaway's name wound up on dozens of Chicago-pressed recordings through his work with the Soulful Strings, the Passions, Syl Johnson, Garland Green, the Five Stairsteps, Little Milton, and other artists. For most of that time, he had yet to release a solo record:

So, one day, Donny came and he said, "Sidney, I just cut a record called 'Ghetto,' 'In the Ghetto.' You gotta hear it." So, we played it, and I said, "Donny, this is a monster." He said, "You like it, you sure?" So, anyway, a little while later, he came back and he said, "Sidney, they're putting the record out. Looks like it's going to be a big record." And we sat there and actually cried together. Because . . . nobody gave him recognition.[9]

"The Ghetto," Hathaway's breakthrough hit, was recorded in 1969 and released the following year. His debut album, *Everything Is Everything*, was mastered in May 1970 and released that July on Atlantic Records' ATCO subsidiary. The iconic "This Christmas" came together at producer and Impressions' lead singer Jerry Butler's Songwriters' Workshop, with music by Hathaway and artful lyrics by Nadine McKinnor and Hathaway.[10] The now-standard soul Christmas carol was recorded in Chicago during the fall of 1970 and released in time for that year's holiday season. However, the signature arrangement with buoyant horns, slinky strings, and a rock-solid Chicago rhythm section traces back to one of Hathaway's earlier arrangements for someone else.

Memphis soul queen Carla Thomas was accustomed to reigning over the charts. "Gee Whiz," her first hit, skyrocketed to the top when she was only fourteen. Her subsequent hits include "Tramp" (a duet with Otis Redding) and "B-A-B-Y." In 1966, she headed to Washington, DC, to begin studies at Howard University along with the then-unknown Hathaway. By late 1969, she was already looking to reenter the music scene and record a new album; simultaneously, Hathaway was starting to make waves in Chicago as an arranger and producer for Curtom Records. Despite having left Howard two years prior, he was brought on to arrange Thomas's untitled album project. One single from the project, "(I'm Going Back To) Living in the City," was released as a single in March 1970.[11] According to the label on the single, Carole King and Charles Larkey wrote the song for the 1969 film *Cactus Flower*, although the recording and composition were not included in the film's soundtrack. In that song, as Carla sang her chorus, the horns punctuated her lines with celebratory bum-bum-bums! And at the conclusion of the chorus, Donny Hathaway's electric piano riffed the now-iconic

buh-duh-duh, buh-duh-duh

The melody was completely different from "This Christmas," but the underpinning was clearly there.

The music industry is a fickle thing; sometimes, releases stall at the gate and are all but forgotten. Sometimes, recorded work is simply never released, left to languish in an unnamed vault. Every once in a while, the best bits of a dead song are resurrected and re-presented. The Carla Thomas album project was inexplicably shelved, and the song was not released in any form except the single. However, the essential arrangement of the chorus of "(I'm Going Back To) Living in the City" (particularly the horn riff) reappeared a few months later in "This Christmas."

Here, the spaghetti-western-influenced horn charts (that according to Ric Powell "was revamped from 'The Magnificent Seven' starring Yul Brynner")[12] gained new life as a festive riff. In the hands of Chicago session players Ric Powell (congas and bass drums), Willie Henderson (saxophone), Phil Upchurch (electric guitar), Louis Satterfield (trombone), and Morris Jennings (drums), the music was rerecorded and reborn. It was injected with fresh energy and zest, ringing in a brand-new conception of Christmas. Years later, lyricist Nadine McKinnor confirmed that though the lyrics of "This Christmas" were born in Black Chicago, she did not intend to reimagine an archetypal Christmas through a Black lens: rather, she was simply writing about her personal experiences of the holiday. She was "trying to capture the swirl of music, department store windows, lights on the South Side—Chicago at Christmas."[13] Drummer, producer, and early Hathaway collaborator Powell confirmed that Hathaway intended to record a Christmas song not simply for his Black Chicago community but to represent and cheer Black culture as a whole. "He knew what he wanted to do musically and the impact he wanted to make with this song. Up until then African-American music wasn't represented in [mainstream] Christmas," Powell explained in 2009.[14] The Blackness apparent in the pores of "This Christmas" comes not from McKinnor's words but from Hathaway's embodiment and performance of them. The song eventually became a Christmas classic, the stylistic antithesis of songs like Bing Crosby's version of "White Christmas," as it manifests an undeniable festivity from the first jingle-bell-laced horn riff to Hathaway's warm string-bathed ad libs at the end, his vocals ringing out a soulful season's greetings. Though "This Christmas" did not appear on an album until 1978's *The Best of Donny Hathaway*, year after year its reputation has grown. It is now a bona fide holiday standard with dozens of covers released in the years since.

A different holiday song produced in Black Chicago around the same time as "This Christmas" explicitly flipped the notion of a white Christmas on its head. "Black Christmas" was written by Chicagoan Pervis Staples (of the Staple Singers) and recorded by fellow Chicagoans the Emotions in November 1970, but the sentiment of the song went back even further.[15] In a December 19, 1965, sermon recorded at Ebenezer Baptist Church ("No Room at the Inn"), the Reverend Dr. Martin Luther King Jr. wished his congregants a "beautiful black Christmas" and spoke about Operation Breadbasket in Chicago, which was celebrating a Black Christmas by giving "black art, black books, and black products as Christmas gifts."[16] The song "Black Christmas" was first performed in 1968 as part of Black Christmas festivities for Operation Breadbasket, and its sentiments reflect those early observances:

> With a black way of living
> A soul way of giving
> This may sound strange,
> But it's gonna be
> a beautiful Black Christmas for me![17]

The lyrics directly echo a statement from a character called the Black Soul Saint of Christmas in a December 1969 article in the *Woodlawn Observer*: "This Black Christmas I shall travel across our city reminding our people that we have a beautiful way of giving and a soulful way of living."[18] The *Observer*, published by the Woodlawn Organization community group, featured a front-page article on the second Black Christmas in 1969. The article described the Black Soul Saint of Christmas as a powerful image that represented the spirit of generosity and consciousness found within the community. The article also outlined a plan by organizers "to control the theological, the psychological and the material aspects of our Christmas" via programming:

> Encouraging Black people to buy their gifts produced by Black people or sold in Black owned stores . . . continu[ing] to develop the Black consciousness of the more than 1.2 million Black people in Chicago . . . by creating

new imagery which expresses the reality that "We Are Somebody," and continu[ing] our development of an atmosphere of love in our community. This includes the spiritual dimension which is the basic meaning of the first Christmas. . . . Just as God gave his son for a new relationship with men, we seek new relationships with our Black brothers and sisters.[19]

After this Operation Breadbasket initiative, people took creative license to use Christmas as a tool to further the ongoing movement toward self-determination in Black Chicago. The energy of Black Christmas had cultural reach far beyond Chicago.

Though the song was born in Chicago, the recorded "Black Christmas" was a Stax affair. The Staple Singers (the group that songwriter Pervis was then a member of) and the Emotions were Chicago-based Stax acts, signed to the Memphis-based label at the time. The record was produced by David Porter and Ronnie Williams of Stax Records, and released nationwide as a white-label promotional 45 rpm record on the Stax subsidiary Volt Records.[20] It was soon banned on some radio stations for being overtly political in a time when racial identity politics were still taboo in some circles. The song did not chart, and original copies are still hard to come by. Three years later, the Emotions would record an equally soulful but less political holiday song for Stax Records, "What Do the Lonely Do at Christmas?," which has also become a soul Christmas standard.

My 1969 copy of *Stax Fax* adds more context to the observance of Black Christmas in Chicago:

> The first annual Dr. Martin Luther King, Jr. Black Christmas Parade was held in 1968. The Rev. Jesse L. Jackson, National Director of SCLC's Operation Breadbasket led the parade from a horse-drawn wagon, symbolizing the poverty of the nation's poor.
>
> More than 90 colorful floats . . . followed the wagon in the two and a half hour parade. More than 80,000 people watched the parade as it went down Dr. King Drive.[21]

The Black Christmas Parade was not the only parade organized by Operation Breadbasket. The Black Easter Parade the following spring gathered over three hundred thousand onlookers around the theme of resurrection, according to *Stax Fax*.

Blacks had earlier flipped a bitter insult into the rallying cry "Black is Beautiful." Likewise, the organizers of the Black Easter celebration adopted the black sheep, a metaphor for scorn and ostracization, as the symbol for the event. The parade photograph appearing in the *Stax Fax* article is stunning: a rather fine black sheep stands in a bed of hay as the float glides down King Drive. The event

> was a success because it reaffirmed blackness and it demonstrated the capacity of the black community to, in fact, resurrect itself from the ghetto to getting together—from a life of despair and the destructiveness of previous conditions to the surge of new life which is ultimately a new existence.[22]

So, along that same stretch of King Drive, nearly fifty years later, a different sort of procession reaffirmed Blackness. Reaffirmed love for our community (if on a much smaller scale). The Black Love Procession, much like the Black Easter Parade, aimed to flip a narrative, though in our case we wanted to combat imagery of Black suffering that was thrust upon us with images of Black beauty and unity.

A few months prior to the procession, Cauleen Smith left an art exhibition at Bronzeville's Black-owned Gallery Guichard by white New Orleanian Ti-Rock Moore feeling markedly disturbed. The *Confronting Truths: Wake Up* exhibition featured a life-size replica of Michael Brown's slain body sprawled on the gallery's floor (also visible from the street through plate-glass windows).[23] After the Ferguson, Missouri, teen was shot and killed by a white police officer in 2014, his slain corpse left splayed in the street under the steaming August afternoon sun, the subsequent grand jury non-indictment sparked massive protests and community-based activism nationwide. The energy was felt nowhere greater than in the surrounding St. Louis metropolitan area.

Smith, then a resident of Bronzeville, Chicago, considered the display of this ghastly image not an expression of art but an act of terrorism against her community. At the very least, it was a traumatic trigger aimed point-blank at an already traumatized population. Black death haunts us from all ends, broadcast on cable news and social media feeds; few places are safe from such energy, and Moore removed art galleries from that short list. Smith wondered what Black artists could do to counteract this visual terrorism. She enlisted like-minded artist friends to strategize a response, and together they decided to organize a parade. Their motivation was simple, as Smith recounted: "we just wanted to tell our folk that we loved them."[24]

The legacy of creativity and collectivity that birthed the Black Christmas and Black Easter parades is part of what kept artist Cauleen Smith in Chicago after a residency brought her to town in the first place.

Once here, she was able to stretch out artistically, also forming deep connections with the artistic community. In her time in Chicago,"[she had] launched parades and wrapped the Hyde Park Art Center in handmade wallpaper; less than two years after arriving, she landed a solo exhibition at the Museum of Contemporary Art that found room for jazz iconoclast Sun Ra, astrophysics, extraterrestrials and Stevie Wonder. She came here as a Sundance-certified filmmaker and left as a filmmaker who also makes sculptures, draws, paints, sews, presses vinyl records, creates puppets and leads marching bands through Chinatown."[25]

That last sentence hints at what happened. She wasn't able to land a lucrative tenured teaching position at any of the local arts schools that would have allowed her to stay where I know her heart was. She wound up leaving Chicago for a faculty position at CalArts in Los Angeles, which was, ultimately, good news for her. But I consider it a loss to Chicago's art community, as well as a personal loss.

Not long before she left town, she mounted a wonderful show called *Human_3.0 Reading List* at the Art Institute of Chicago. It served as a victory lap, of sorts.[26]

The show consisted of dozens of her drawings on graph paper of book covers. In some of the drawings, the artist's hand rests on the book or holds it to display its spine, or just her thumb is visible, pressing down on the corner of a book. The illustrations are of books she felt close to, from Claudia Rankine to Toni Morrison, James Baldwin to Yoko Ono.

Each image replicates the vintage fonts and colors of the original covers, augmented with splashes of watercolor paint and glitter. The work implies a level of care that isn't seen much anymore. It also implies a level of analog connection apropos to the printed word in general. And that level of connection is also a binding element to Cauleen's ever-expanding body of work. She revels in the tangible, whether utilizing analog Sun Ra tapes or sewing scraps of fabric into banners of love and affirmation. I count her a friend and marvel that in everything she does, she does it with energy and connection. She does it with heart.

And I hope, one day, she can again do it in Chicago.

ALL THIS TALK
ABOUT FREEDOM
ART, SOUL, AND THE
BLACKSTONE RANGERS

In about 1968, Chicago author and playwright Useni Eugene Perkins's Free Black Press published *Our Voice: Poetry by Black Children* (fig. 5). That book contains the following poem about the Blackstone Rangers (a pow-erful South Side Black gang) written by the then-eleven-year-old Patricia Lathion:

> Black Stone Rangers
> . . . Black, Raw, Ready
> Sores in the city
> That do not want to heal.[1]

The poem is striking because it implies a latent energy among the youths that is untapped, right alongside the view that these young people were somehow damaged "sores in the city." The question, however, is whether it is true that they "do not want to heal." Or is that assertion a symptom of society's ongoing discount of young people who've gotten entangled in gang life?

In 1967, members of the Blackstone Rangers collaborated with singer-composer-playwright-activist Oscar Brown Jr. to create a musical revue called *Opportunity Please Knock*. About eight thousand people attended the

FIGURE 5. Front cover of *Our Voice: Poetry by Black Children*. (Author's personal collection)

show during the first weeks of performance at Chicago's First Presbyterian Church. The show gave exposure to various teens with ample talent but little opportunity.

In the mid-1960s, Brown produced a show called *Summer in the City* at Harper Theater in Hyde Park (on the South Side). It wasn't doing well there, though it had been a hit on the North Side. After investigating, he discovered that his patrons were afraid of the Blackstone Rangers, who hung out around 53rd Street.

Oscar Brown Jr. noted in a 1996 interview that

> the fact that there was this gang presence was bad for business and that's one of the reasons that I contacted gangs—could we do something for them that would stop them from steppin' on my hustle! I said we'd do a show for 'em, but they said, "well, we got some talent, can we be in the show?"[2]

The gang's proposal seemed to counter the completely negative impact that most people assume gangs have on communities. The contradiction was fleshed out in a 1969 article by James Alan McPherson:

> Since the emergence of the Ranger Nation, individual members have been charged with murder, robbery, rape, knifings, extortion of South Side merchants, traffic in narcotics, extortion and intimidation of young children, forced gang membership, and a general history of outright violence, especially against the Disciples who never joined the Rangers. On the other hand, the Ranger Nation has been credited with keeping the South Side of Chicago "cool" during the summer of 1967 and the spring of 1968, following the assassination of Dr. Martin Luther King. It has been said that they have kept drugs, alcoholics, prostitutes, and whites hunting for prostitutes out of their neighborhoods. . . . They have been alternately praised and condemned by the national press, their community, the United States Senate, the local police, and Chicago youth organizations to such an extent that, if one depends on the news media for information, it is almost impossible to maintain a consistent opinion of the Blackstone Rangers.[3]

Much of the Blackstone Rangers' nefarious activity stemmed from economic necessity. To that end, *Opportunity Please Knock* wound up being mutually beneficial. The young people got a platform to display their talents, earn some profit, and Oscar Brown Jr. noted that he was impacted, as well:

> It let me see that there was this enormous talent in the black community. This is where all the dances came from; this is where all the popular music comes from; so I began to really concentrate on that. *Opportunity Please Knock* ran for a little while, with those kids being on the *Smothers Brothers Comedy Hour*.[4]

In another article about the revue, Brown observed that

> these kids are angry because they're being shot through the same grease
> their parents were shot through, and they understand that it's impossible
> for a bootless man to pull himself up by his bootstraps. But they're not too
> disillusioned to work hard—if they ever had any illusions at all. It is up to
> us to give them a better picture of reality.[5]

Maggie Brown, Oscar's daughter, told me on *Reclaimed Soul* that "in the
news in those times they were just saying those young black boys were just
rats . . . and he said, 'no they're not rats—they're our children and they're
beautiful, and they have talent . . . and those talents can come to their own
economic rescue.'"[6]

The creation of *Opportunity Please Knock* was truly Afro-optimistic en-
trepreneurism and imagination in their purest forms.

Two songs from the show, "All This Talk about Freedom" backed with
"I'll Be Back" (a Vietnam War–themed number), were released on jazz
pianist Ramsey Lewis's very short-lived independent record label, Ramsel,
in 1968.[7] Besides the televised performance (which journalist Carol Marin
asserted was staffed not by Rangers but by "the people [Rangers leader]
Jeff Fort sent to LA to sing on the *Smothers Brothers Show*")[8] and a feature
in *Ebony*, very little archival evidence of the performances remains.

Meanwhile, on the West Side, the Conservative Vice Lords (CVL) caught
wind of the project. According to Maggie Brown, they "sort of kidnapped"
Oscar briefly and strongly suggested he work with them on a project as well.
He obliged.

During this time, the CVL, who had officially incorporated and reformu-
lated themselves as a street organization rather than a gang, were concen-
trating on enterprising hustles that married culture and entrepreneurship.

This period is documented beautifully in DeWitt Beall's 1970 *Lord Thing*.
In the film, CVL spokesman Bobby Gore affirms the state of mind behind
the organization's shift:

> For everything that happens, there has to be a reason. The way we live, the
> food we eat, the amount of money we got in our pockets. If none of this is
> suitable, then we're gonna leave home with an attitude. If we really look at
> things for what it's really worth, our problem is really not among ourselves.
> Because the things that we argue and fuss and fight over it's not coming

from us, it's coming from environment. . . . The brother is not his problem, the problem comes from somewhere else. So, what we're trying to create here, is let's find out where our problems are coming from.[9]

By 1969, the organization had partnered with the Museum of Contemporary Art to create a storefront community art center called Art & Soul. In 1968, two days before Dr. Martin Luther King Jr. was assassinated, they opened a Tastee-Freez ice cream parlor franchise. They also established the African Lion, a boutique specializing in African-influenced clothing and accessories.[10]

Jet covered the opening of another enterprise, the Lion's Den club.[11] The magazine ran an image of the Staple Singers performing at the opening celebration in a vacant lot, Pops Staples's guitar glistening in the sun. A large mural that I surmise is by Don McIlvaine (a prolific West Side–based artist who taught at the CVL's Art & Soul center) looms in the background.

In *Lord Thing*, Kenneth "Goat" Parks, a CVL leader, states at a press conference,

We're dealing in two worlds: one black and one white. . . . the have and the have nots. But the guys over here and the Vice Lords, the people over here in the Lawndale area want their piece of the pie. And they willing to do their homework . . . to get it. They're willing to handle it. There's a lot of money that can be invested and it isn't. It's being sidetracked. It never filters down to the grassroots level. It never gets it. I mean, look around! If it got here, where is it now?

An unnamed member of the press asks him: "Have you been involved in any of these killings? Or any of the murders? How do you stop the killing?"

Parks responds: "How do you stop the killings? You stop the killings by giving the people an investment in their community. By making the people here know that they are a part of each other. That by destroying each other, they're not going to solve their problems."

All this may seem totally improbable: that even gangsters in Chicago got caught up in Afro-optimism. The immediate assumption might be that gangsters are a strictly nefarious force in a community. But, such improbability is absolutely true to the spirit of Chicago's creative energy: an audaciously expectant, forward-leaning energy drenched liberally with a desire for self-determination.

These were not the only experiments of Chicago-based entertainers connecting with the raw talent around them. By 1970, soul singer Jerry Butler (along with help from Gene Chandler), had organized his Songwriters' Workshop. The workshop consisted of up-and-coming talent: songwriters, producers, and vocalists, who were allowed the freedom to woodshed their ideas under the tutelage of more seasoned soul stars. They experimented with jazz idioms and sophisticated themes. They honed the Chicago sound.

Jerry Butler, along with other Chicago artists of the time, felt as though the tides of soul were shifting. His fruitful partnership with Kenny Gamble and Leon Huff in Philadelphia had dissolved, and he was, in a sense, on his own. In a 1970 article, Butler espouses that

> Black Music is . . . getting into politics, it's getting into things that really touch people other than just the things that effect them in their homes. I've always felt that "soul" music is "people" music.[12]

Around this time, Jerry's friend singer Gene Chandler was also taking charge of his own career. He began producing his own records, and out of the gate had a million seller with "Groovy Situation." Chandler also revamped the small Bamboo label out of St. Louis, and started his own imprint, "Mister Chand" Records. He joined me on the radio in 2008.

> I had been in the business since the latter part of 1961 when the Duke of Earl came out. As I went along in the business, I decided I wanted to have a record company; cause I always had a business mind, thinking in that direction.
>
> When I originally started my record company, I was young, of course, and thought that I was going to be able to get Eugene Record [chief songwriter and lead singer of the Chi-Lites], and Curtis Mayfield. At that time, he didn't have Curtom, his record company. Before I could close the deal, Curtis went and started his record company, and Eugene Record ended up staying with the Brunswick people [the label that released the Chi-Lites' material at the time]. And now, I'm stuck with all of these acts [Simtec & Wylie, the Popular Five, Krystal Generation, et al] to produce on my own. I didn't intend to do it by myself, but that's the way it ended up.[13]

In regards to his signature song, "The Duke of Earl," he shared that he gets writing royalties and performance royalties, but not publishing royalties. It was an early lesson Chandler learned about the business.

He told me that "At the time I wasn't smart enough to know about publishing companies." But Chandler figured it out soon enough.

Another 1970 article was tellingly titled "Chicago—To Build a Creative Soul Center." In the piece, W. Yale Matheson, attorney and advisor to Butler and Chandler, explains that

> you have half a dozen, already established artists, as well as writers and producers, all of them with the possible exception of Jerry, under 30— Gene [Chandler], Curtis Mayfield, Bobby Miller who produces the Dells, men like this—who are determined to build themselves within this environment of Chicago. They've all had marked success and they're not anxious to leave this town, they have faith in the talent potential, and are well financed and well organized and absolutely determined to do everything from here.[14]

Jerry Butler's workshop was initially affiliated with Chicago-based Mercury Records. The momentum to build a soul center in Chicago resulted in a valiant effort, rooted in a desire for self-determination and a track record of success.

He launched the careers of songwriters Terry Callier and Larry Wade, James Blumenberg, and later, Zane Grey and Len Ron Hanks (among others). Grey and Hanks had a couple of disco hits, "Dancin'" and "You Fooled Me," and wrote a smash for LTD: 1976's "(Every Time I Turn Around) Back in Love Again."

What the movement for a soul center could not have foreseen, however, was the mass exodus of the music industry from Chicago, which ultimately struck a blow that the workshop could not overcome.

But these records remain. And this energy remains. And the inclination toward self-determination remains strong, bubbling up in Black Chicago's creative scene generation after generation. It is the yearning for self-determination that's behind Chance the Rapper's phenomenal rise to success without being signed to a record label. And the story begins again and again.

BLACK

Gene Ford[,] Oakenwald South, Room 104–5[,] 11 yrs.
. . . Black's not bitter,
Black is sweet.
If you are black don't be ashame,
Because black is a beautiful name.[15]

IT'S A TOM TOM, PART 1
TAMALES, BARBECUE, AND 45S

Culture, especially Black culture, is a moving target. Ever-evolving, the idea of purity within Black culture is strictly a myth. The myth of purity is applied to Black culture by cultural gatekeepers who don't understand that, by our very nature, we create from what is already before us, constantly remixing and reworking ideas. Part of the allure of Sly Stone's *There's a Riot Goin' On* is that even as the drum machine–propelled sound of the songs has a perpetual degree of momentum, the ghosts of previous recordings reside in the master tape. He reused the same tapes over and over again, resulting in a murky sonic quality.[1]

I think that gatekeepers who are preoccupied with determining and maintaining "purity" or "authenticity" in Black music and culture have a deep misunderstanding of the core of Black culture. Black culture at its heart is both pulling from our past and forward leaning.

In the cases of both jazz and hip-hop, improvisation shows up prominently (in hip-hop, it's known as freestyle). Every exclamation of "that's not jazz" or even "that's not hip-hop" ignores the African trait of constant remixing, of improvisation as being instrumental to our culture. The very birth of hip-hop is rooted in the remix. Every record is pregnant with the possibility of a radical rearrangement. But that's something that hip-hop also shares with jazz: every night at the club, a composition has the possibility of being reborn in the musicians' deft hands. Unlike the classical Western music tradition that's reliant on replicating what is transcribed on sheet music, jazz hinges on using sheet music as a jumping-off point. The culture is a muddied, moving, beautiful target.

According to the artist Arthur Jafa, "Black people figured out how to make culture in freefall."[2] We are constantly rebuilding, sometimes due to calamity, but usually as a result of necessary ingenuity, pulling from the ghosts of what's come before us to use as source material for a fresh thing. And it's those deep-seated roots, a tethering between past and future, that add complexity to Black invention.

Here in Black Chicago, that forward-and-back lean is evident in our music, and even in two of our ubiquitous carryout dishes: barbecue and tamales. Each of those dishes, and even the industry built up around them, is rooted in the notion of making culture with what was available, despite the circumstances.

Blues songs from as far back as the 1920s tout the "hot tamale man," reflecting the dish's presence in Chicago (and the American South), even though the very idea of Chicago tamales may sound blasphemous.[3] But there are not one but two such creatures, each wholly different from a traditional Mexican *tamal*.

I have memories of my grandmother (born in Chicago in 1916), boiling Tom Tom tamales in their distinctive white wax-paper wrappers on her avocado green stovetop. Machine-made since the late 1930s, the Tom Tom tamale has more in common with a hot dog than a traditional tamale. The soft cornmeal cylinders filled with beef or soy are often available at Chicago hot dog stands. No familiar corn husk. No shredded meat.

And then there's the Mississippi Delta tamale that made the Great Migration to Chicago along with so many other children of Mississippi. Another riff on the Mexican tamale, again featuring cornmeal rather than masa. These are cradled in corn husks but feature a spicy red broth.

Barbecue is another culinary tradition that traveled to Chicago from the South. By the 1950s, barbecue pits became far more ubiquitous in Black Chicago than tamale stands. And they even began to eclipse in sheer numbers traditional sit-down restaurants that served southern fare—hot biscuits, and shrimp and crabs—the sort that advertised "Home cooking our specialty" in the *Chicago Defender* back in the 1920s and 1930s (long before such restaurants used the term "soul food"). But while those southern cafés aimed to serve customers a taste of home, barbecue's migration to Chicago begat something altogether different, borne mostly out of necessity.

٭ ٭ ٭

Argia B. Collins and his brothers formed a Collins Barbecue empire of sorts beginning in about 1951. But eventually he secured a deal to get Mumbo Sauce into grocery stores alongside household named sauces like Open Pit.

Argia also invested in his community: creating a South Side manufacturing plant at West 91st and South Halsted Streets, and he even bankrolled soul singer Garland Green's stint at the Chicago Conservatory of Music.

Argia B.'s family lived in a small apartment above the plant. Back in the 1960s, according to Allison Collins, Argia B.'s daughter, "we'd pour warm bottles of barbecue sauce off the assembly line. Throughout the neighborhood you had the aroma of Mumbo Sauce just kind of clinging in the air."[4]

These families took a tradition begun in Mississippi and reimagined it here in Chicago. Restrictive city ordinances prevented the traditional means of smoking meat over an open flame indoors, so barbecue pitmasters had aquarium cookers (so called because of their resemblance to aquariums) custom-made. The cookers were primarily fabricated by Leo Davis, beginning in 1951.[5]

The enclosed cooking process results in concentrated smoky flavor and particularly moist meat. And, each huge, see-through glass and steel device served as the heart of a miniature economic engine.

The resulting barbecue spawned a number of dynasties, including the one run by the Collins family. Though the Collins Barbecue restaurants are all closed now, Allison has kept her father's Mumbo barbecue sauce alive, a metaphor for so many of our treasured cultural artifacts.

Allison told this story to my radio audience in April 2008:

> My father . . . was a South Side restaurateur in Chicago in the early 1950s. . . . Mumbo Sauce was something that he wanted to do to set his restaurants apart. And the sauce, in a sense, also served as a conduit within the community.
>
> For my father, this process took place during the '50s and '60s. That had a lot of implications for African American business owners. I think what he

realized was "this is a business that I can develop, I can employ people from the community." And that's exactly what we did. We had a small manufacturing plant. I have two sisters and a brother, and we all were involved. It was a family business, but it was also a neighborhood business when we initially started out.

The people that he recruited initially to help him were folks from the neighborhood who needed jobs, often high school students that were out of school for the summer, looking to earn extra money.

The first factory was his restaurant. My dad ended up with three restaurants. He started out in Bronzeville, which is a neighborhood in Chicago. The first manufacturing plant that I remember was located at 9350 South Halsted. It was a conveyor belt where we'd . . . bottle the product, label it. Box it up.

Mumbo Sauce also served as a signifier, for some, representing alliances within the Black community.

Lloyd King, a musician and educator who grew up in near-suburban Oak Park, Illinois, in the 1960s and '70s also talked about how his family embraced the sauce on my radio program: "Mumbo. It really starts with my old man, you know, my father. He was a 'race man,' as they used to call him back in the day. He was all for the Black people getting their voice, getting their power, so he wanted to use Black businesses. But I remember the sauce, and I thought it was the only kind of sauce there was. And I remember you'd go over to the white kids' house and they'd have Open Pit. And I didn't even know . . . what was this Open Pit? To me, barbecue sauce was Mumbo. If it didn't taste like Mumbo, it wasn't really barbecue sauce."[6]

* * *

According to Allison Collins, Argia B., like the rest of his clan, was always looking for the next logical step forward in business. And he also believed in supporting the community through his business. So, for Argia B. to take a leap by sponsoring a neighborhood singer was not so unusual. After all, just as barbecue has served as an economic engine in Black Chicago, so has the music industry.

Garland Green once told me that in the 1960s he was a fixture at the South Side talent shows that local record executives scoured for fresh talent. He made a name for himself as a growling, burgeoning baritone to be reckoned with. His performances of Chuck Jackson's "I Wake Up Crying" were his ace in the hole. With that song, he said, "he could never lose."

Ironically, he wasn't discovered at a talent show, but playing a game of pool.

When Garland arrived in Chicago from Mississippi, he lived at 6510 South Yale Avenue, in Chicago's Englewood neighborhood, with his brother, Wilbur Green. According to Garland, "[Argia B. Collins] heard me singing in the pool room on 63rd and Normal, and he had a barbecue place right next door. And he came over from his business just to hear me play pool and sing. And it just really thrilled him. He asked me if I would like to pursue a singing career, and take voice and piano. So he financed that."[7] Argia B. funded Garland Green's education at the Chicago Conservatory of Music in the late 1960s.

Garland went on to record dozens of sides for various record labels. He hit it big in 1969 with "Jealous Kinda Fella." Like his wager on the profitability of Mumbo Sauce, Argia B.'s bet on a promising young singer proved to be a successful endeavor.

In the 1960s, as barbecue restaurants were hitting their stride in Chicago, dotted abundantly across the South and West Sides like fat marbled in beef brisket, the popular recording industry in Chicago (occupied primarily by blues, soul, jazz, and gospel, and to lesser degrees rock, pop, and what was then called "ethnic" music) was booming. Home to larger labels like Chess and Mercury, independents like USA, One-Der-Ful, and Vee Jay, and featuring label outposts for ABC-Paramount and Brunswick, the soul scene in particular was studded with hitmakers, and South Michigan Avenue, known as Record Row, was buzzing.[8] The record business, not unlike barbecue, was a scalable enterprise. Whether the label was situated in the back of a record store on the West Side or a high-rise downtown, there was a chance for some money to be made in trade for a black plastic disk. Artists, producers, and songwriters were akin to prospectors, hoping to strike gold with the right combination of sound and lyric. Session musicians like Phil Upchurch zipped from studio to studio, playing a blues riff for Jimmy Reed one session, and a gospel riff for the Staple Singers the next. In between, playing sets on the vibrant local club circuit, and lucrative jingle sessions for advertising firms like Leo Burnett kept kids in diapers and talent honed for vocalists and players alike. Fortunes rose and fell on the next big hit.

But by the late 1970s, most labels in town had either gone out of business or decamped and headed for the coasts. One of the biggest losses was the sale and ultimate implosion of Chess Records, which, not unlike the Collins family's constellation of barbecue enterprises, was a family affair, begun by Leonard and Phil Chess in 1950.[9]

Chess was the home to a variety of the most archetypal Chicago music stars during their artistic zeniths. Their roster included Muddy Waters, Little Walter, Howlin' Wolf, Koko Taylor, Ahmad Jamal, the Dells, Etta James, Bo Diddley, the Soul Stirrers, Jackie Ross, Fontella Bass, and Ramsey Lewis among many others. It was also home to deeply influential arrangers and producers like Willie Dixon, Gene Barge, Richard Evans, and Charles Stepney.

In many ways, Chess served as rock 'n' roll's bassinet. The so-called first rock recording, "Rocket 88" (credited to Jackie Brenston [who was actually Ike Turner] and His Delta Cats), was released on Chess in 1951.

And generations of rockers have drawn inspiration from Chess recordings by Bo Diddley (like "Who Do You Love"), Chuck Berry ("Maybellene," "School Days," "Back in the USA"), and of course the bevy of electrified delta blues that emanated from the label.

❧　❧　❧

In 2006, Marshall Chess, son of Chess cofounder Leonard Chess, spoke with me on *Reclaimed Soul*.[10] His story is of particular interest here because it's reflective of the inventive energy that was bursting at the seams of late 1960s Chicago. It also reflects that Chess Records, during its apex, was a family business at its core, and he saw himself squarely fitting into that legacy, echoing Allison Collins and the Collins barbecue enterprise. Lastly, Chess was a family-run label that was arguably the antithesis of the corporate recording industry behemoths that were to come. That's not to say that large record companies didn't exist in the mid-twentieth century, but the industry had not yet reached its current state, in which the vast majority of recorded product—past and present—is controlled by only a few corporations. Chess was a relatively small and independent company even at its peak. Still, it had an outsized influence on American popular music broadly and in particular a deep impact on Chicago's sonic culture. From the inception of their company, Leonard and Phil Chess laid down on wax and distributed the electrified Delta blues that would become one of Chicago's most enduring calling cards. But by the mid-1960s, Leonard's son, Marshall, was in his mid-twenties and dreaming of the next chapter of influence.

In 1967, Marshall Chess had an idea.

I'd been born and raised in the record business, I wanted to do my own thing, Now, I was part of that sixties "sex, drugs, and rock 'n' roll" movement that everyone my age was. And, I got the idea to start my own conceptual label. And the family had no problem. I mean, basically I had the keys to the recording studio, so I could do what I wanted at night. I got the idea for this album, but the name actually came from me and a gentleman named Roland Binzer who was a young advertising whiz in Chicago back in 1967. He had a very avant-garde ad agency called Hurvis, Binzer, and Churchill. He was doing some advertising work for us at Chess, and for our radio station, WVON, and I met him. And we came up with this name "Rotary Connection." I thought it was a very catchy name.

Beloved singer Minnie Riperton (then an unknown session singer) and seasoned industry insider Sidney Barnes were charter members of Rotary Connection. Minnie (fig. 6) had been born and raised in Chicago, and Sidney was a new transplant to Chicago most recently from Detroit, where he worked with George Clinton, among others. I spoke with Sidney in 2007 on *Reclaimed Soul*.

They had the riots in Detroit. [Fellow recording artist and producer] Andre Williams . . . I was hangin' out with him at the time. Andre and I went out for Chicago, because I wanted to be with Chess Records. That was one of my goals in life.

So, we got there and they signed me up as a writer, producer, artist. And I started writing and working with people like Muddy Waters, Bo Diddley, and the Dells. Marshall came to us one day, Minnie [Riperton] and I. Minnie was a secretary at the time. [Minnie had also recorded for Chess as a part of a girl group called the Gems.]

She had had a record out as Andrea Davis. It did okay.[11]

FIGURE 6. Minnie Riperton promotional photo, circa 1974. (Author's personal collection)

That recording was her first solo outing: "You Gave Me Soul" backed by "Lonely Girl." The B-side is a dreamy, soulful waltz, awash with moody strings that ebb and flow dynamically. It showcased her signature whistle register during its chorus. Sidney continued.

> I was doing a little writing and producing. [Marshall Chess and Charles Stepney] said "we want you two to help us put together this little concept thing." And, it was just a studio act. And the record came out [in 1967]. I think on the original recording it was me, Minnie.... Chuck Barksdale of the Dells was one of the singers, too. And [there were] three other people that were local white artists ... they just did bar mitzvahs and things.

According to Marshall Chess, the other members of the studio group were from "a white rock-and-roll band" called the Proper Strangers, who had recorded a few sides for a small indie label called Quill Records.

Sidney Barnes explained that Marshall "wanted the white sound [and] the soul sound together.... And the thing took off, you know!"

One of my favorite Rotary Connection albums is *Songs*, a collection of compositions by artists as varied as Stevie Wonder and Eric Clapton. Sidney explained: "When we did the *Songs* album we were big. We had just come off the road with Janis [Joplin], we had played with the Rolling Stones. We had done the [Texas] International Pop Festival by then. We were feeling really powerful." When we spoke, Sidney suggested I listen to "We're Going Wrong."

The song is fronted by Minnie Riperton, who produced a characteristically stunning performance for the cover of a song originally performed by Cream. Her whistle register makes an appearance. Sidney explained:

> I would be on stage with her sometimes when she was having a good night, and she'd hit some of them notes.... People would just stop and just stand there and stare, because they couldn't believe that was coming out of that little girl standing on the stage. She was incredible.
>
> And she didn't want to do that at first, because when she first started as Andrea Davis, she was playing these little night clubs, and people said, "we don't want to hear that shit! That opera shit! Don't be doing that! Sing Aretha Franklin!" So, she had stopped doing it [on stage].
>
> We'd mess around and she'd do it, so we wanted her to do it on the album, [Charles] Stepney and I. And, she didn't want to do it. So, we forced her to

do it. And she did it on the first album. . . . Everyone around the studio was starting to get knocked out by it, because by then, rock 'n' roll was coming in and people were doing all kind of things.

So, when we did our first gig [as Rotary Connection], she did not do it at all, because she was afraid. So, we used a theremin.

Marshall Chess told me that he had heard the theremin on the Beach Boys' smash record *Good Vibrations*. He recognized it as "a strange electronic instrument that was invented in Russia." Before this point it was perhaps best known as a staple sonic element to all manner of creature-feature B-movies and TV shows.

Marshall went on, "I was able to get one in Chicago, and I became a theremin player, you know? I patched it into this big amplifier."

So, according to Sidney, "Marshall came on stage and played the theremin. And after the show, Minnie said, 'Shit, I can do better than that!' And I said, 'You do it, girl. You do it.' And [after that], she would do it. Audiences were much more responsive then the hecklers Minnie faced years before. Sidney hinted that part of the reason for their openness was that "people, were taking acid then."

Marshall Chess served as producer or coproducer on nearly all of the Cadet Concept releases. In addition to the Rotary Connection, he most famously released dramatically psychedelic blues recordings by Chess stars Howlin' Wolf and Muddy Waters. On *Reclaimed Soul*, he explained how he picked the roster for the label.

How does a manager of a baseball team pick the players, you know? This guy at second base, this guy here. . . . It was my baby, it was my whole life at that time.

I loved the first [self-titled] Rotary Connection album. I loved the two albums I did with Muddy Waters, called *Electric Mud* and *After the Rain*. And I did one with Howlin' Wolf that I really liked, too. An electric psychedelic album all with the same band. Another album I loved on Cadet Concept was called *Blowin' Gold* by John Klemmer, which is one of the first fusion jazz albums.

But all these albums used this great group of studio musicians that I put together, along with the help of Charles Stepney and Gene Barge. I don't want to leave him out. Gene was a producer at Chess Records. And he helped a lot. You know, we put together this group that we felt were the most avant-garde, hottest musicians at the time in Chicago. Morris Jennings on drums, who later played with Ramsey Lewis. Louis Satterfield on bass. [Later on] he was the trombone player and the bass player with Earth, Wind & Fire. Pete Cosey on guitar, who then was discovered by Miles Davis, and played on Miles Davis's electric albums [Cosey joined Davis's band in 1973]. Phil Upchurch, the great guitarist, who's still a fabulous, well-known jazz guitarist.

So, we put together this fantastic rhythm section . . . with the help of Charles Stepney and the help of Gene Barge. And the biggest help was me having the keys to the studio, so we had a place to work . . . create. Then, we added to that Charles' great arrangements, and brought in these fantastic classical musicians from the Chicago Symphony on strings and the great horn players. And we ended up making some unique and original records that . . . people are still asking about, as you are. It held up.

It was in the midst of that creative peak that the proverbial bubble burst: Marshall's father, Leonard Chess, died suddenly in October 1969. Marshall explained:

I come from a family of immigrants. My father and uncle came from Poland to the United States, and I began very early—even twelve or thirteen—going to Chess Records. I wanted to be around my father, and they were glad to have me there sweeping the floor, getting coffee, loading trucks, packing boxes. So, when Chess Records was sold [after Leonard Chess's death], I was highly disappointed because my whole life, that's what I wanted to do. It was like taking an Olympic event away from an athlete after he had trained for ten years to be in it. But, I quickly recovered from that. I ended up founding the Rolling Stones' record label [in 1971], and spent seven years running their business.

This is notable because, early in their career, the Rolling Stones made a pilgrimage to Chess Records to record an album in 1964. Even their name is in direct homage to Chess recording artist Muddy Waters's 1950 song "Rollin' Stone." Additionally, pivotal Chess Records producer Gene Barge (also a gifted saxophonist) toured and recorded extensively with the Stones, beginning in the late 1970s.

Chess Records was sold to General Recorded Tape (GRT), a manufacturing company with no experience on the creative side of the recording industry. GRT was disastrously hands-off. Chess Studios fell into obsolescence, and it wasn't long before the label lost its dominant stature on the scene. The slow decline of Chess that began in the early 1970s was compounded by the continued shuttering of the smaller labels and production companies around it, some of which had rented Chess Studios for their own recording needs. Meanwhile, some of the larger labels with satellite offices in town, like ABC and Columbia, simply pulled out of Chicago all together. But it wasn't just the labels that left town. There was also a significant talent drain, arguably beginning around the time of Earth, Wind & Fire's exodus from Chicago in 1970. Founder Maurice White had deep ties to Chess Records—he was a session drummer there beginning in the winter of 1964, playing on dozens of records like Billy Stewart's slow jam hit, "I Do Love You," and the Fontella Bass smash "Rescue Me." Louis Satterfield, perhaps best known as a horn player, played bass alongside Maurice White on many of these recordings.[12] Later in the decade, he recorded for the label as part of the Ramsey Lewis Trio with bassist Cleveland Eaton. This period was transformational artistically for Maurice, who notes in his biography that "if Chess Records was college, the Ramsey Lewis Trio was [his] PhD." He closely observed Ramsey Lewis's flair for stage presence, musicianship and his consummate professionalism. Notably, Maurice first performed on stage with a kalimba while still in Ramsey's Trio (at Ramsey's insistence). The kalimba, which White picked up after watching Phil Cohran play it at the Affro-Arts Theater, later became a signature instrument for White. He even named his production company Kalimba Productions.[13]

When the first iteration of Earth, Wind & Fire left Chicago for the West Coast, they were newly formed, with a sound forged from the horn-heavy sounds and Afro-centric rhythms that were en vogue on the Chicago scene of the time, but they had not yet attained the stratospheric fame that was to come. And though they left the city, members of Earth, Wind & Fire continuously intertwined creatively with Chicago-based artists throughout the 1970s, during the apex of their fame, recording with Chicago-bred talent like Deniece Williams and the Emotions, and counting Chicagoans such as Don Myrick, Wade Flemons, Rhamlee Michael Davis, Yackov Ben Israel, Sherry Scott, and Maurice's brothers, Fred and Verdine, as members at one time or another. Exploring that particular web of creativity is a means toward understanding the energy and interconnectivity of the Chicago scene during this period.

Earth, Wind & Fire represents an era when the self-contained soul-funk band was the norm. In the 1970s, bands like Tower of Power, War, Parliament/Funkadelic, and even Rufus (a band that began in Chicago out of the ashes of rock group The American Breed) were multimillion-dollar draws that filled arenas (as the expansive ranks of their bands filled stages). And, Earth, Wind & Fire was right on the cutting edge of that trend from their infancy. However, according to Sidney Barnes of Rotary Connection, their initial template was born even earlier in Chicago.

Earth, Wind & Fire formed around 1969, at the height of Rotary Connection's fame, and according to Sidney Barnes, they patterned themselves after Rotary.

> When they first saw us, Maurice [White] was still playing drums with Ramsey Lewis [on Chess's Cadet Records subsidiary].
>
> We were all with the same label. . . . We did a show at that college on the South Side [Chicago State University], and it was Ramsey Lewis and Rotary Connection.

Beyond being labelmates, the links between the two groups were myriad. Ramsey Lewis and Rotary Connection were both being produced by Charles Stepney, and Rotary Connection's Minnie Riperton sang background vocals on a number of Ramsey's records from around this time, including an early version of one of her signature songs, "Les Fleurs," which was on Ramsey Lewis's 1968 album, *Maiden Voyage*. Minnie recorded her own version of the tune on her debut solo album, 1970's *Come to My Garden*, an album that Maurice White played drums on during his time in the Ramsey Lewis Trio.

According to Barnes,

> Ramsey and his group [a trio then consisting of Ramsey and Maurice White, rounded out by bassist Cleveland Eaton; see fig. 7] had never seen us [live], they were doing jazz. The crowd when we went on went *crazy*. So, Maurice said, "That's what I want to do. I was thinking about leaving Ramsey, and I didn't know what I wanted to do; but that's what I want to do." . . . He wanted Minnie and I to join with him. And we didn't. So, what happened was [around the time that] Rotary broke up, he formed Earth,

THE GENTLE-MEN OF JAZZ
Featuring
RAMSEY LEWIS, CLEVELAND EATON, MAURICE WHITE

FIGURE 7. Ramsey Lewis Trio promotional photo, circa 1968. Left to right: Cleveland Eaton, Ramsey Lewis, Maurice White. (Author's personal collection)

Wind & Fire, which was originally called Salty Peppers. And he got Charles Stepney, and he got Jessica Cleaves.

Cleaves was a high soprano from the soul-pop group Friends of Distinction. Before Jessica, the female member of the group was Sherry Scott of Chicago, whose equally sweet voice was not nearly as high. She was a founding member of the band who wrote and led an early EWF hit, "Think about Loving You."

According to Sidney, "[Maurice] wanted what Rotary had. His beginning stage show was exactly [like Rotary's]. . . . I played congas, so Maurice was playing congas, and Minnie sung high, so he got somebody to sing high. Charles Stepney was our arranger, so he got Charles Stepney."

The major difference was that Rotary Connection was completely integrated in a time when an integrated rock and soul band was revolutionary. As Sidney recalls, however, Maurice "wanted it all-black, so he got the horn section [a unit known as the Phenix Horns] that he always had with them." That unit basically evolved out of the Pharaohs, which had come out of Phil Cohran's Artistic Heritage Ensemble and had often played at Cohran's Affro-Arts Theater in the late 1960s.

The origins of Earth, Wind & Fire's extensive use of Egyptian iconography can be traced back to their roots as the Pharaohs. The Pharaohs released one album (*Awakening*) on Scarab Records during their original iteration. The orange, gold, and white album has numerous Egyptian references on its sleeve, and the back cover relates an origin story dripping in self-determination:

> Once upon our time there is a group of young men who came together and formulate a dream.
>
> They dared to dream that they could create an approach to the arts that would encompass their experience in America, the soul of their mother land . . . Africa, and the spirit of the oneness of the universe. This marked the "AWAKENING."
>
> . . . listen to the sounds of the Pygmies blended with the Soul Sounds of 39th Street in Chicago . . . PYGMY POWER! Listen to the sounds of "FREEDOM" . . . listen to the simultaneous dimensions of time (past, present, future) in the "GREAT HOUSE" . . . listen and you shall hear the spiritual fruits of the "PHARAOHS."[14]

The Phenix Horns had a pro-Black, fiercely independent edge that was not unique on the Chicago music scene of the time: the AACM was founded in 1965 by now-legendary musicians Phil Cohran, Muhal Richard Abrams, Steve McCall, and Jodie Christian, although Cohran left the group early on. Even today the AACM remains fundamentally committed to the expression of creative or free Black music, both ancient and future.

Some fifty years later, the AACM still bears fruit featuring multiple generations that uphold the credo of "A Power Stronger than Itself": from original members of the Art Ensemble of Chicago, bassist Harrison Bankhead, vocalist Dee Alexander, and sitarist Shanta Nurullah, to flutist Nicole Mitchell, bassist Junius Paul, and trumpeter Ben LaMar Gay.

The sonic and thematic DNA of Earth, Wind & Fire is made clear when you hear a song like the Pharaohs' "Freedom Road." Thumpy, aggressive staccato horns dominate. A hopeful chorus rings out: "Freedom. Oh Freedom. / Freedom down in my soul!"[15] From there, listen to a Rotary Connection song like 1971's "I Am the Black Gold of the Sun." The song was cowritten by Charles Stepney and Richard Rudolph (Minnie Riperton's husband and artistic collaborator). "I am a man . . . so free! (I am the Black Gold of the Sun!)"[16] Compare that to Earth, Wind & Fire's 1973 hit "Keep Your Head to the Sky," which closes out with Jessica Cleaves's whistle register. Here, strings, guitars, and rhythm propel the music forward: "Gave me the will to be free / Purpose to live is reality."[17] "Black Gold" was arranged by Charles Stepney, who went on to arrange Earth, Wind & Fire signatures like "Reasons," "That's the Way of the World," and "Can't Hide Love." Those classics wed a percussive horn sound with string, rhythm, and guitar elements, bound together with an underpinning of analog synthesizers (which were cutting edge at the time).

Even though Earth, Wind & Fire was part of a cohort of artists who left town at the dawn of the 1970s, their sound was continuously refreshed by Chicago energy. Most conspicuously, from about 1973 until his untimely death in 1976, Charles Stepney was instrumental in crafting the EWF syncopated horn sound. And starting around 1976, Maurice White's old friend Tom Tom Washington (see the next chapter) continued the thread of the group's Chicago connection with arrangements for songs like "September." Additionally, EWF's Maurice White coproduced work by his old mentor and bandmate Ramsey Lewis, as well as for the Emotions and Deniece Williams. Much of that work was recorded at Paul Serrano's PS Studios.

Both the Emotions and Deniece Williams were initially based in the Chicago area and had recorded since the 1960s, but neither act reached superstardom until their association with Maurice White's Kalimba Productions began in the mid-1970s. That association bore fruit such as Deniece Williams's breakout hit, "Free." Drawn from the stellar 1976 album

This Is Niecey, "Free" was coproduced and arranged by Charles Stepney, who tragically passed away before the album's release in the fall of 1976.

Kalimba Productions was also responsible for a string of five albums by the Emotions. Those albums included Emotions perennials "Don't Ask My Neighbors" and "Best of My Love." The first album in the sequence, *Flowers*, was released the week before its arranger, Stepney, died.

I mention the timeline of Stepney's death in relation to these albums to illustrate that he was arguably at the peak of his abilities when he died. Charles Stepney's arrangements still sound like freedom, wide as a horizon, levitating over yesterday, careening toward an unseen tomorrow. Hip and untethered, his sound was born during a time when Black humanity was focused on building a new world. Universally lauded in Chicago's music scene, his death at the age of forty-five was keenly felt.

Earth, Wind & Fire's *Spirit* album, released in September 1976, was co-produced and arranged by Stepney, as well. The orange-and-black inner sleeve of the LP contains a dedication written by Maurice White:

> With every band, the departure of spirit must take place. It is a destiny that is inevitable. We, EARTH, WIND, & FIRE, were blessed to have had a gifted spirit work among us. He had now departed to the next plane. He left us with much beauty and inspiration for humanity to feed upon. The works in this album [which includes hits "Getaway," "On Your Face," and "Imagination"] are dedicated to Brother Charles Stepney (1931–1976). May God embrace his spirit with love.[18]

Though many artists left Chicago in the 1970s, some, like Peabo Bryson, were still being drawn from elsewhere to record here by Chicago's sterling record of hitmaking. Two of Peabo's breakthrough hits, "Reaching for the Sky" and "Feel the Fire," were recorded and produced in Chicago with proven hitmakers Richard Evans and Gene Barge (each formerly of Chess Records), and the Chicago-based songwriting team of Chuck Jackson and Marvin Yancy (who were once members of the gospel-tinged soul group, the Independents). Peabo was from the same hometown as Chuck Jackson and Marvin Yancy: Greenville, South Carolina.

Chuck and Marvin had an enviable stretch of hits in the 1970s crafting tunes for Natalie Cole (including "This Will Be," "Our Love," and the Chicago soul classic, "Annie Mae"). They set the stage for her ascent as an international pop star. Natalie happened to also be Marvin's wife at the time. The couple made their home in Chicago during the mid-1970s; and, though her father, the legendary Nat King Cole, was born and raised in Chicago (and she had familial ties here), Natalie was a West Coast girl at heart. In a 1977 interview on WJPC, Chicago radio legend Richard Steele asked Cole if she had moved to Los Angeles. She waffled: "Mmmhmm. Back and forth."[19]

Richard asked about her husband and quipped that "the collaboration of Marvin and Natalie Cole has not only produced a child, but a new album." She was being interviewed to promote *Thankful*, a new album that coincided with the birth of her only child, Robbie Yancy. The album was her last that was primarily recorded and produced in Chicago. During the interview, Steele asked Cole if she wrote music, as well:

> Well, I don't really consider myself a writer; but, somehow or another I was able to get together a couple of tunes the last two albums. . . . This last one I was really pleased. A song that I wrote that I kept under my hat for like two years, which I wrote right here in Chicago is on the album. That's called "Keeping a Light." And then, I cowrote "Lovers," and also cowrote another song called "La Costa" with my piano player, Linda.

Natalie was referring to singer-songwriter Linda Williams. Linda recorded a lovely album called *City Living* with an all-star cast of session players, some sessions taking place in Los Angeles and some in Chicago.

Natalie also mentioned in her conversation with Steele that she wrote a song by herself on *Thankful* titled "Annie Mae." That song wound up being particularly popular in Chicago. The song was produced by Chuck and Marvin and was arranged by Chicagoans Richard Evans and Gene Barge. Though both Evans and Barge were Chess Records alumni, their sounds represented two ends of the Chicago soul spectrum.

By this point in his lengthy career, Gene Barge had crafted archetypal recordings for blues and gospel artists like Little Milton, Etta James, the Soul Stirrers, and the Meditation Singers. Meanwhile, Richard Evans specialized in string-heavy jazz recordings like his signature work by the Soulful Strings, and his work with pianist Ahmad Jamal, jazz harpist Dorothy Ashby, and vocalist Marlena Shaw. Gene Barge and Richard Evans's collective work in the late 1970s represented the continuation of the Chess sound and energy, as well as a melding of two inextricably linked threads in Chicago music: blues and gospel, and soul and jazz.

Despite Cole's recording success in Chicago, she never truly acclimated to the city, and by 1978, she had essentially returned to the West Coast.

However, many Chicago artists, like Tyrone Davis, Walter Jackson, and the Chi-Lites, chose to stay.

Another of the artists who stayed in Chicago during this time was the legendary bluesy soul singer Otis Clay. In the 1970s, more artists were taking creative control (and in some cases, complete control) of their recording careers. I spoke in 2013 to Clay on my radio show. In his career, he had recorded for a number of labels during the 1960s and through the mid-1970s. But after a particularly bad experience in which he essentially "didn't get paid" while under contract (according to his longtime friend and collaborator Tom Tom Washington), in 1975 Otis started his own label, Echo.

It was kind of unusual for me to being doing that at that time to say, well you know all of these other people . . . had really been messing up my life, so now it's my turn. . . . And I decided that in late '74. . . . So, when I moved into the office down on Michigan, heart of Record Row, 2131 South Michigan, all the guys stopped by and said 'okay man, what are you doing?' [I said] 'Well, hey, you know, I'm gonna record myself. And, all the people . . . the writers and everybody was coming around. . . . We had a small studio there. So we were all standing around and started writing things.[20]

His first single on Echo (a cover of Tyrone Davis's smash "Turn Back the Hands of Time" backed by an original funky blues stomper, "Good Lovin") did well enough to be picked up for national distribution by Elka, a larger label.

I asked him how he'd gotten to that place.

I got to that place because . . . you hear all the stories, and you go to a producer's house and you sit around his pool, and he got all the drinks with the little umbrellas in it and they say "Everything's gonna be alright. Don't worry. This is it, here." And that's *not* it.

I was coming off of some records . . . I got caught in the shuffle because my last label was Hi Records.

Hi Records out of Memphis was most famously home to Al Green. The label was singularly invested in the promotion of its biggest star, who'd cracked the lucrative pop market wide open. Their fixated investment was sometimes to the detriment of Hi's more blues-oriented artists (including Otis Clay, Ann Peebles, and Chicago's own Syl Johnson).

Clay went on:

I wasn't angry . . . I was just at that point where I said "I'm gonna do some-thing, I'm gonna do this." That was the straw that broke the camel's back. And October of 1974 was when Pervis Spann [longtime disc jockey and eventual owner of legacy radio station WVON], who was my friend . . . more than anything . . . and manager, said "you know, your contract is up with Hi Records . . . and they want to know what you're going to do." And I said, "I'm not going to do anything. . . . I'm not signing with anybody else. . . . I just want to go and do things that I'm happy with."

And, you can rest assured, when you're doing it on your own, you won't go to bed mad at night. [*Laughs.*] Because, you can easily forgive yourself.

Peace emanates from self-determination.

IT'S A TOM TOM, PART 2

IRON SHARPENING IRON

Black Chicago absolutely hums with music. Drifting down from apartment windows in the summer: Philip Bailey of Earth, Wind & Fire perpetually crooning "I'll write a song for you, / You'll write a song for me, / We'll write a song."[1]

A man sitting on a lawn chair, listening to the Best of Tyrone Davis blasting from his indigo-blue pickup parked at Rainbow Beach in South Shore, children playing with a beach ball in the calm teal water that seems to go on forever. It is everywhere, an inextricable thread of our cultural fabric. And so many of those songs, so many of those threads, are tied to one man: Tom Tom Washington.

In my crate digging, I actually look for his name on a record as a mark of excellence. I call it looking for a Tom Tom. I have at least a few hundred cuts he's had a hand in—under the names Tom Tom, Tom Tom 74, Tom Tom 75, Tom Tom 84, Tom Tom Washington, and a variety of other aliases. Tom Tom Washington also branched out and worked with artists from all over the world, including the Whispers. The Whispers are a Los Angeles–based group, and in 1978, he did arrangements for an album titled *Headlights*. I know this because at one point I found a 45 rpm single taken from the album. I'm not usually a fan of the Whispers, but it's a beast, featuring the top cut, "Olivia (Lost and Turned Out)" (which is about exactly what you think it's about), and on the B-side "Try and Make it Better," which is bangin'. The tunes' arrangements capture the distinctive sound that Tom Tom made classic on songs like "Serpentine Fire" by Earth, Wind & Fire. The 45 is amazing. But why wouldn't it be? It's a Tom Tom. His music is an enduring example of what happens when creative energy and a signature sound are cultivated over many years: it becomes more evident, more idiosyncratic. Unlike so many of his contemporaries, he chose to stay and hone his craft in the scene that nurtured him, even as the pillars of the Chicago music scene began to crumble. What does it mean to stay, after you have nothing left to prove? And what does it mean to be fully invested in continuing the transfer of creative energy to the next generation? Tom Tom's work as of late has been tied up in demonstrating the answers to those question.

It was the summer of 2010. I was privileged enough to hear the iconic (and prolific) arranger Tom Tom Washington play a few chords of the tune "There'll Come a Time" on a piano stationed at Soundmine Recording Studio on 80th Street and Stony Island Avenue, where in the vacant lot next door cabbage was growing. The experience was electric, especially because Betty Everett's "There'll Come a Time" (released in 1969 on Uni Records) was one of the first Chicago Soul albums I ever owned. It was also exciting because Tom Tom Washington arranged some of my favorite cuts on the album (we later both agreed on our favorite: "1900 Yester-day," sort of an off-kilter swinging '60s dance cut). On the album, Betty's sassy-yet-classy salty mezzo-soprano voice was perfectly augmented by swirling strings, staccato horns, shuffling doo-wop background vocals, and rollicking piano. Featuring compositions by Eugene Record (of the Chi-Lites), Curtis Mayfield, and Eddie Sullivan (of the Classic Sullivans), the album is a snapshot of Chicago soul at the time.

As a Chicagoan and a music lover, Tom Tom Washington's distinctive horn and string arrangements are like home to me.

Arrangements are essentially everything you hear in a record outside of the vocal melody, and serve as supportive counter-compositions to the song itself. In some cases, the most hummable part of a recording is a horn riff or a guitar lick, but neither of those elements of a track are actually considered a part of the song itself. This is why the Grammys have categories both for Song of the Year (which considers strictly the main composition of a song) and Recording of the Year (which considers the track in its totality, including the arrangement).

A signature element of Tom Tom Washington's arrangements is his use of over-the-top orchestral flourishes that he calls his "fanfares." These call the listener to immediate attention. You can hear such a fanfare at the top of Gene Chandler's million-seller "Groovy Situation" on Mercury (then a Chicago-based label). It manifests itself in the first few moments of glorious Tyrone Davis B-side on Brunswick Records, "You Wouldn't Believe." These make me break into a smile because often the fanfare has little kinship to the song itself or even to the rest of the arrangement. Sometimes, it serves as a recurring hook, but other times it stands alone at the front end of the song: a little thirty-second showpiece before the record settles into the undeniable flow of the groove.

Tom Tom came up in Chicago's Ida B. Wells projects and studied music under the tutelage of James Mack (an awe-inspiring arranger in his own right). He wound up arranging dozens of records for Chicago music heavyweights, among them Earth, Wind & Fire, the Emotions, Tyrone Davis, Deniece Williams (who is from nearby Gary, Indiana), the Staple Singers, Ramsey Lewis, Leroy Hutson, the Chi-Lites, Otis Leavill, the Lost Generation, Betty Everett, Jerry Butler, and Loleatta Holloway.

In fact, a deeply abbreviated list of songs that he's arranged could serve as a Chicago Soul songbook:

"Get On Up"—Esquires (1967)
"The Sly, Slick, and the Wicked"—Lost Generation (1970)
"Oh Girl," "Living in the Footsteps of Another Man"—Chi-Lites
"Love Jones"—Brighter Side of Darkness (1972)
"The First Time We Met"—Independents (1973)
"Serpentine Fire," "September," "Love's Holiday," "Fantasy," "I'll Write a
    Song for You," "Be Ever Wonderful"—Earth Wind & Fire (1978)
"Best of My Love," "Don't Ask My Neighbors," "Rejoice"—Emotions
    (1977)
"Can You Feel It," "Heartbreak Hotel"—Jacksons (1980)[2]

And he even arranged a number of classics that are not otherwise connected to Chicago, including the horns on *Face Value* and *... But Seriously* by Phil Collins.

I want to reiterate that this is a very abbreviated cross section of Tom Tom's work. He is as prolific as he is humble.

Otis Clay noted:

> Some of my friends left, and was going out to California on a project and never came back (chuckles). I don't know how Tom Tom [Washington] didn't get caught up in that. [Arranger and guitarist] Benjamin Wright went out to do a thing . . . for Motown with Bobby Taylor and the Vancouvers and he never came back. [Saxophonist, writer, and producer] Monk Higgins, who also went out there to do a project . . . he never came back.[3]

In the late 1970s and into the 1980s, clubs on the South and West Sides that supported live music began to shutter. Coupled with the wholesale scale-back of the recording industry in Chicago, the classrooms where so many musicians had learned their craft were becoming things of the past. This wasn't simply a sign of the times, moreso a small slice of an overarching trend of disinvestment in these communities.

In Jamaica, an abandoned property very quickly returns to the earth. Weeds and wild things take hold with a vengeance. There, this is called ruination, which sounds disastrous, but in some ways, it isn't so. Yes, thick ropes of vines and fruits and all manner of creature might take hold there, and so-called civilization might be blotted out, but out of ruination comes creation. Out of elegant decay comes the necessity for remix. Likewise, despite disinvestment and abandonment, the ground of the West and South Sides of Chicago is not fallow. Rich culture is still in full bloom, only lacking the infrastructure that in decades past helped cultivate it.

One of the most consistent hitmakers in Chicago's classic soul scene, Tom Tom would not (or could not) let that tradition of collective cultivation go. And so, the South Side Community Big Band, Tom Tom's exercise in autonomy, was born.

His idea to create a big band that plays his original, world-class arrangements and that plays exclusively on the South Side arose from a realization that the music that he and his colleagues had created was not theirs. Or more accurately, they (and their community) were not reaping the benefits it.

North Side club owners and record label conglomerates are the primary beneficiaries of Black Chicago's music legacy. With fewer and fewer live music venues in Black communities, the organic (nonacademic) means of passing the music and the energy to the next generation are, according to Tom Tom, in jeopardy. And he's prepared to do something about it.

I talked to Tom Tom Washington and Gene Barge after a rehearsal of the South Side Community Big Band. We were at Soundmine Recording Studios, which stands just south of 79th Street and Stony Island Avenue on the South Side, a few blocks south of Mosque Maryam and a few blocks north of where Curtis Mayfield first set up shop for his Curtom Records. It's also just south of the former High Chaparral lounge, a Black-owned club that was one of the most popular on the South Side throughout the 1970s. In some sense, it's the perfect location for an exercise in self-determination.

TOM TOM WASHINGTON: Well, Chicago. . . . Back in the day, we had all kinds of venues where we could hone our skills. In other words, we had joints. Not so much that everybody wanted to go play and hang out, but that's how you learned how to play music. You'd emulate what you saw. Well, the young kids today, what do they see? They don't see anything, so they don't learn anything, you know? What we learned is not in school. So we need venues and places for people to perform, and they're not always on festivals and things. We've had intimate settings where there are fifty or sixty people, and they're close up. Where they can communicate with the people and the musicians. You know, sometimes you get sixty thousand people in the audience at a festival, you would never get a chance to talk to me or him. [*Laughs.*] . . . So, we need venues, and we need venues on the South Side. Everything is North. People go all the way up to the North Side to listen to something that's South. It's crazy.

This band is called the South Side Big Band, so it's dedicated to playing on the South Side.

We live on the South Side. This band, playin' what we're playin, you gotta come to the South Side to hear it.

This is where everything was at. . . . In the beginning, everything was on the South Side. We've got some substantial places . . . but we have to create them.[4]

The producer and saxophonist Gene Barge works and plays with Tom Tom through the big band. They've been colleagues on the scene for fifty years. Barge is involved with the project because he strongly believes in its mission.

> GENE BARGE: It's our music and it was stolen from us in terms of the financial rewards. In terms of the credit. So what we're doing here with this orchestra . . . is we're trying to reassert ourselves to show the city of Chicago that "hey, we're not just going to let you take the music from us," you know?
>
> Tom's out front crawling and scratching. . . . We're trying to reassert ourselves so we can gain some of the recognition, and let some of our younger people (and other people) see what we are doing.

Earlier that evening in the studio I caught snatches of conversations between other horn players. An older saxophonist convening with a player scarcely out of the conservatory. A thirty-something trumpeter chuckling with a sixty-something trombonist. Many players mentioned that the variety of ages represented that night was a unique and important characteristic of the band. So, I asked Tom Tom and Gene to talk about the intergenerational nature of the Big Band.

> TTW: If we don't show the younger people what we've learned, then they will never learn. This is not in textbooks.
>
> GB: First of all, a lot of the guys you saw sitting out there tonight are in education. We have a lot of people sitting there. Curtis Prince [an accomplished jazz drummer and educator with a career spanning over fifty years]. Burgess Gardner's son, who's got his master's . . . who plays with the orchestra. [both trumpeter Derrick and his brother (trombonist Vincent Gardner) are accomplished players, composers, and educators who have recorded with artists like Lizz Wright and Wynton Marsalis and for their own projects]. He heard about the band, his daddy [Burgess] tells him about us . . .

Burgess Gardner is a prolific producer, arranger, player, and songwriter. Pivotal on the Chicago scene for decades, he worked with Monk Higgins,

Chuck Bernard, General Crook, and others. Notably, he also produced and arranged for a small suite of labels (More Soul, Lamarr, Down to Earth) co-owned by his brother, Walter, in the early 1970s.

GENE BARGE: A lot of the young musicians on the road today were taught by a lot of the guys you see sitting in this room. Tom and all of them mentored a lot of the young musicians that are playing with what you would call the star acts . . . or headliners. . . . What we've been trying to do is keep the involvement and evolvement going with some of the younger players, but we're fighting a tough battle.

[Quincy Jones] will tell you that he learned in the pool parlor. What he learned, he learned from other musicians. He didn't get a chance to go to conservatory. . . . A lot of our best musicians learned from other musicians. Learned in the streets. Learned on the set. Hanging out in the clubs. Jam all night. "Try to get into [recording and jam] sessions, so I can hone my skills."

We got a combination of guys who didn't get the formal training who are damn good, and then we got the guys who got the formal training who are also damn good.

Guys who scuffled, couldn't afford lessons. Couldn't afford nothing. Couldn't afford a horn or a piano in their house.

That's what we got going on in the black community, we got people . . . it's a miracle that some of them can play.

TOM TOM WASHINGTON: I don't know any soul people who got formal training.

I asked them, "What about arranger James Mack? He taught many musicians at Crane Junior College?" James Mack was classically trained and arranged for artists like Peabo Bryson and Natalie Cole. According to Tom Tom (who attended some junior college classes taught by Mack but never earned a degree), James was an exception among most of the Black players of his generation.

TOM TOM: We came from the University of the Streets. Like he [Barge] said, iron sharpening iron. Willie [Henderson] went to Phillips [High School, home of a famous music program helmed by Walter Dyett]. We come from the streets. That's how we learned the music. The kind of things that we learned in school, from a technical standpoint, we can't use none of that stuff out here.

85

Singer Reggie Torian Sr.'s story is a classic example of the process of "iron sharpening iron," the transferring of energy that Tom Tom talks about, and how the network of clubs in Black Chicago served as both training grounds and a means for local talent scouts to discover fresh, young artists.

Reggie grew up in the south suburbs of Chicago in the 1960s, listening to Major Lance, Walter Jackson, and the Impressions on the radio—all music written and produced by Curtis Mayfield here in town. He was a member of the Impressions (fig. 8) for decades, singing the falsetto lead after Curtis vacated the role. I spoke with Reggie in 2013, several years before his death.

REGGIE TORIAN SR.: In the eighth grade or so I really started zoning in on the Temptations and the Impressions. So, at night, when I'd go to bed, I'd put on the Impressions album, and the speakers were under my bed. And it'd just play all night. When I'd wake up in the morning, it'd be playing. So, when I got the offer to audition for the Impressions [in 1972], I thought they were kidding. 'Cause now we're talking about some ten years later, and I'm trying to break into the field in Chicago. And we're at the High Chaparral.

AC: [*Softly*] By "we," you mean the Soul Enchanters.

RT: Yeah. The Soul Enchanters.

AC: I got you.

RT: [*Pleased*] Aw, listen at you! [*We both chuckle.*]

RT: . . . And, so, we're doing dates in Chicago. Young people nowadays think you have to get paid for everything that you do. Man, wherever they would let us sing: the Green Bunny, the High Chaparral . . . where we were basically the house band; we'd just go in, have the opportunity to sing, and hope someone [would] discover us.

And it was at the High Chaparral's venue, with Clarence Ludd. He knew the Impressions were looking for a replacement for Leroy Hutson, who had replaced Curtis and was there for about eighteen months. And so, he agreed to lease me, or lend me to them for six months till they could find a permanent lead. Because the Soul Enchanters had a song [1973's "A Fool Like Me" on Jimmy Vanleer's Golden Ear Records, produced by Clarence Ludd with Johnny Moore]." Reggie's distinctive falsetto set him up perfectly to replace Curtis.

The irony is that I always loved the music. And I loved the Curtis Mayfield music. So, when the opportunity came up, I knew all the Impressions' songs. There were very few things they could name, that Curtis Mayfield wrote [that I didn't know].[5]

Later in our conversation, I played Reggie my copy of "This Loves For Real," from *Times Have Changed*, the last Impressions album featuring Leroy Hutson. The song was written by Leroy Hutson, who had produced and released another version of it by a group called the Hands of Time on the tiny Inner City Records imprint. The Impressions version was released around the time that Reggie was being onboarded into the group, and features Leroy's lead vocals gliding between falsetto and tenor backed up by emotive strings, percussive horns, and a particularly haunting woodwind riff.

REGGIE TORIAN SR.: [That song] just reminds me of the snow and the cold, and the long drive in from Wentworth Gardens in Chicago Heights to Sam [Gooden] and Fred [Cash]'s houses on 87th near the expressway.

IMPRESSIONS
ON CURTOM RECORDS

MGMT:
(312) 769-4676

FIGURE 8. Impressions promotional photo, circa 1974. Left to right: Fred Cash, Ralph Johnson, Reggie Torian, Sam Gooden. (Author's personal collection)

AC: And they all look alike. All those houses are still there.

RT: And they lived next door to each other. So, we'd go down in Sam's basement, and Sam would run me through the drill night after night. And Fred would come peek his head in, then go out to Curtom, working on the *Preacher Man* album [a Rich Tufo–produced concept album, *Preacher Man* is the only Impressions album with lead vocals mostly by Fred].

But that period of time, when you're in transition, from mediocrity . . . and you're about to step into a great group . . . and the word is out that you've done it. The media has printed it. But, you haven't performed, you haven't drawn a paycheck. There's this waiting, and that wondering, and that longing: "Is this really going to happen?"

'Cause when I joined them, I was in this complex called Wentworth Gardens in Chicago Heights. And the *Chicago Heights Star* had published a picture. . . . I joined the group in August of '72. In April, they did this article and everybody's wondering, you know, when they gonna see me on TV? When am I gonna move out of Chicago Heights? And I had all this pressure.

I'm driving this ugly, beat-up Electra 225. Supposed to be a four-door, but it's only got three. [*We both laugh.*] It was that period. And then, I just remember Leroy's voice, because he hadn't left yet. He was still performing with the group. [I was] wondering, when is he going . . . to leave?

And finally, one January, they went out to LA, and he decided that would be his last performance [with the Impressions], at the Santa Monica Civic Center. So, they flew me out, and that's when we did the television shows. We did, I think it was *Midnight Special*, *Soul Train*, [and] *American Bandstand*.

And, now, it's time to move. It took a while, but you just have to continue to have faith and hang in there.

In the final years of his long career with the Impressions, Reggie helped develop and starred in *It's Alright to Have a Good Time—The Story of Curtis Mayfield*, a popular stage show that ran at the Black Ensemble Theater. In 1990, Mayfield suffered a tragic accident that left him a quadriplegic; Torian's portrayal of a paralyzed Curtis Mayfield garnered critical acclaim. Reggie also developed and headlined a musical revue called *All Things Mayfield*.

Generational transitions within cultural institutions have a tendency to bring with them a certain level of turmoil. But in the case of the AACM, its ability to thrive over fifty years after its founding has been directly tied to its decision to pass the baton.[6] But that decision was less than unanimous, at first, and also less than easy.

Bassist Junius Paul was born in Chicago in 1982. An AACM member, he currently tours the world with Roscoe Mitchell and the Art Ensemble of Chicago, as well as a number of younger groups (including his own quartet). In many ways, he is a bridge between the legendary founders of the organization and the new thing.

The founders (who included Roscoe Mitchell, Steve McCall, Jodie Christian, and Baba Phil Cohran) were all fairly young when the AACM was formed in 1965, so it was ironic that a certain turmoil arose when a number of folks in their twenties (including Isaiah Spencer, Corey Wilkes, Justin Dillard, and Junius Paul) wanted to join the AACM in the early 2000s. It was by then an institution, and perhaps the older members were protective over what they'd spent decades building. It was also ironic that most of the people who were most vocally against the younger generation being officially folded into the group were not from the founding AACM generation, so they themselves had been brought in at some point by older cats.

Fifteen years later, Junius Paul explained to me what happened.

I get it now. At the time, when you're young and you just want to get in . . . And, you can't really see that aspect of it . . . it's just, "why?" . . . We want to be a part of this thing. We feel like, as the younger blood, we can push it along, so what's up? We're ready to be under your tutelage. This ain't, like, no takeover. We're trying to come in and learn, you know? I still don't agree with it, but I understand.

But, there were those few [in the AACM] that saw differently [from the dissenters], and weren't afraid to say it; and they spoke up for us. And that was huge.

[Saxophonist] Ernest Dawkins has a lot to do with that, as far as bringing the young cats in. He was one of the people that saw the vision. He was another one that spoke up for us, big time.[7]

Dawkins was of the second generation that joined the AACM in the mid- to late 1970s and the 1980s. After many of the original members of the AACM (like Anthony Braxton, Richard Muhal Abrams, and the Art Ensemble of Chicago) decamped for France or New York in the 1970s, the second generation played a crucial role in keeping the Chicago roots of the group both solvent and vital.

I would argue that some of the main advocates for onboarding younger members in the 2000s had been marginalized within the organization, women (like Mama Ann Ward and Nicole Mitchell) in particular. I point this out not to villainize this revered organization, but it's important to recognize that the group was not immune to the societal norm of misogyny.

Too many Black-built institutions—in Chicago and elsewhere—suffer from founders' syndrome. Founders are unwilling or unable to pass the baton, and the inevitable result is death and decomposition.

Yet, despite some earlier internal struggles, the AACM is one of the few organizations that appears to be successfully passing the torch. It is a multigenerational, creative entity that is still relevant, vibrant, and exciting. Younger members are continuing the tradition of pushing the envelope, rather than riding the coattails of the fifty-year-old group's reputation.

Junius notes that "once we got in, we represented." Hailing from Chicago, he followed the timeworn pattern of iron sharpening iron, or learning his craft primarily in the clubs with older musicians who supported the transfer of energy. Additionally, he learned playing in the church, another common trait of musicians and vocalists here.

In October 2002, as a young, hungry musician, Junius began going to Velvet Lounge. The Velvet was founded in 1983 by one-time AACM member Fred Anderson. The fabled jazz saxophonist's club served as a conduit for the transfer of energy between generations through its Sunday night jam sessions.

Junius, Justin Dillard, Corey Wilkes, and Isaiah Spencer were among the young cats who came to the jam sessions at that time. This was sometime before any of them joined the AACM, but it set the scene for what was ahead for them.

Junius recalled that he "started working around the city from the Velvet Lounge." It was a place to be heard. He also got connected with members of the AACM from the sessions. And, he had many experiences that fundamentally changed him.

It's like in Africa or something. If you had this society of diviners or medicine people, or you know, sages or whatever you want to call it. It's this thing. And you don't really talk about it a whole lot. The Velvet stuff is not secret; but there are certain aspects of it . . . if you weren't there, you weren't there.

'Cause you can't even go back to that area to imagine it anymore, because the whole area has changed.

The Velvet Lounge moved from 2128½ South Indiana to 67 East Cermak and was sold in 2010 after Fred Anderson's death. The Cermak address no longer hosts jazz sessions. Once a fruitful space for creative music, 2128 South Indiana is now the address of a gleaming building stacked with high-priced condos.

In my conversation with Junius, I offered: "I don't want to get blasphemous, but it sounds sort of like a religious experience. In Tulsa, I attended a small storefront church. Just a little joint, but it was so imbued with the spirit, that I can't explain it to people. People don't know. I can't even go to a church anymore that doesn't feel like that. It completely changed my definition of what a house of the Lord is supposed to feel like."

"Mhhmm. Mmhmm. Mhhhmmm. Yeah," Junius affirmed, then continued:

And you don't know until you experience it. And when you experience it you can't go back. That's the Velvet Lounge. It was very much like church. I had some unbelievable spiritual experiences there. You can feel this thing inside of you. There were moments at the Velvet Lounge that were so magical that I'd get scared. I remember a night with [drummer and AACM member] Vincent Davis. It was like, oh my God. He can play with that intensity for that long. The Velvet Lounge was the first time I experienced anything like that. I didn't think that people could do that. And it scared me. You think you've heard some shit . . . and then you hear something that completely destroys anything that you thought you knew.

Those Velvet Lounge jam sessions also shaped who Junius became as a musician.

The wallpaper, everything. The vibe of the Velvet Lounge. The old chandeliers. What I learned from the Velvet, and the people I was able to be around, and the music I was able to play, and the things I was taught. All of that. What was encouraged. We were encouraged to be ourselves at the Velvet Lounge. . . . And those were my beginnings of learning that it's okay to be what you are and who you are as an artist and a person. It's cool. You don't have to fit into anything if you don't want to. Matter of fact, we don't even want you to fit into what you don't want to fit into.

And the Velvet Lounge really helped to spark that curiosity of, like, trying to find the people and the artists who made their own rules and succeeded.

What they taught me is that you can be yourself, as long as you're badass at it.

What is right now with me has so much to do with the Velvet Lounge. That wallpaper lives on, man. Fred [Anderson] lives on. And just everything we all learned from the Velvet Lounge as youngsters. We are that now. We are the Velvet Lounge.

After a pause, I added, "There's a difference, though, between the spirit and the mind. In the sense that there is an intellectual aspect to playing the music, but there's also a spiritual thing. And when we talk about something that you can't learn in school, maybe part of that is the spiritual aspect. And I think about this a lot. 'The music' has sort of been coopted by the academy. So, you can go to school to learn 'the music.'"

"Yes, there are classes . . ." He trailed off.

"They teach you the notes, but they don't teach you the spirit," I clarified.

"That's the biggest issue I have. Like anything else, they tried to marginalize to this academic thing," Junius paused. "People have fetishized blues music. People come to Chicago and want to get this blues thing. People forget there's lifestyle that went into that playing. And that's why a lot of the stuff now doesn't sound like it did then. Because spirit comes from your life and how you're living."

Ben LaMar Gay is another AACM member on the younger end of the organization's spectrum of players. The South Side native is also a cornetist who embodies the traditional blues griot, but with a decidedly twenty-first-century twist: he's as comfortable with a diddley bow as he is with a Roland 808 synthesizer. His recordings and performances reflect the adventurousness that's the calling card of fellow AACM members Anthony

Braxton, Rene Baker, and one of his heroes, Richard Muhal Abrams. When I hear him, his playing squeezes my heart like a lemon. Lemons are one of the most sugar-rich citrus fruits, but the sweetness is girded in complex, sour undertones. He's also a seasoned storyteller, as when I asked him about the links to both past and present in his music:

> Basically, I'm a man. I'm from Louise, who raised me on the South Side of Chicago. I'm just this kid that used to play on the block.
>
> And, at one point, the fire hydrant would go off. We'd play in the water. We would play running bases . . . strikeout. . . . But, there's this one particular moment when this man, if you can imagine someone that looked like John Lee Hooker on a ten-speed with a boombox, and he's bumpin' the blues hardcore. And all these activities on this block pause . . . because he had to get through that block groovin'.
>
> And so, with that tradition, I'm just one of the kids that stared at the bluesman a little bit too long as he turned the corner. As he grooved off our block. And so, in the mid-part of my process of just being a person trying to learn something, I run into different members of the AACM who are just other citizens of the city with different stories. And, with that tagline: ancient to the future, you can just throw it up in the air and not worry about what falls first, ancient or the future. . . . I am a South Side bluesman, really. But I'm attempting to toss things in the air, and they can fall in whatever order they wish to fall in.[8]

Ben notes that being from Chicago contributes to his identity as an artist in other ways, as well.

> When you're born and raised here, there's a certain toughness . . . just dealing with natural conditions of this area. And then being by that huge, inland, freshwater . . . sea . . . Lake Michigan, but it's a weird sea. Being next to that water. . . . There's something about just the energy of this area, that sometimes attracts people. [There's] all this documentation that people create from being here . . . let's just say just albums, you know, from these generations of people. Not only just the AACM. I think maybe, if you just like vibrate inside the center of where you're from, and let it be honest because this is where you're from. If you get right down to the nucleus and vibrate with it, things will project. And so, I think that's what I'm attempting to do.

To me, the energy that Ben refers to (and the energy that he so clearly demonstrates) dances between the desire to innovate, and the feeling of being tethered to what's come before. Watching Ben LaMar Gay at the Chicago Overground Showcase in New York City's 2019 Winter Jazzfest was akin to watching something being born.[9] He performed an otherworldly version of Chuck Berry's "Maybellene" (originally recorded in Chicago back in 1955). In the hands of Ben and his band, with a tuba bassline and his unmistakable vocals, it was as if the roof was torn off the club and the inky-blue sky and stars enveloped us.

That showcase was revelatory for me. Each group that performed consisted primarily of Chicagoans, with a smattering of ex-pat Chicagoans. I hosted the showcase at a Lower East Side club called Nublu, and standing on stage, I found myself having to articulate this energy in real time to people who had never even been to Chicago. What was this thing? As I suggested to Julian Reid—a pianist and member of Juju Exchange, a soulful jazz collective fronted by trumpeter Nico Segal—sometimes teaching someone else helps clarify your ideas.

After graduating from Chicago's Whitney Young High School, Julian went on to Yale. His study of gospel music traditions has led to feelings of deep connections with his predecessors. After the showcase, we made plans to reconvene our conversation in Chicago. I spoke with him on a spring morning in 2019. He was full of verve.

JULIAN REID: Just in the waters is Thomas Dorsey who started so much of what we know now to be Gospel. He popularized it. . . . Right here in the city at Pilgrim Baptist. And so, being in between gospel and jazz, I feel all of those legacies trickled down from new cats who are close to my age, to elder statesman, to people have passed on even before I was really aware of anything. Like Dorsey, and that is such a cool legacy to steward, and also to learn more about as you get older. So I've been doing a lot of research lately on Gospel and Gospel in the city and how it came about and how that was connected to the Great Migration coming up from the south. So all of this is flowing through my veins literally and musically.[10]

I thought about how when I heard Julian play keys as part of the Juju Exchange with his high school friend and collaborator Nico Segal, his chords drew clearly from gospel's well.

I smiled, thinking back to when we'd met, in the wake of that performance.

AYANA CONTRERAS: I said to you, "you play in church." I feel like that might have been the very first thing I said to you.

JULIAN REID: [*Nodding*] I think that's right.

AC: Yeah, because some of those chords you were using, I was like, *Gospel*.

JR: Yeah. I love it.

AC: But, I think a lot of folks who are listening to the music coming out of Chicago from specifically your generation, like mid-twenties-age folks, notice that there is a pretty strong gospel influence in a lot of [your] music, from Jamila [Woods] and Chance [the Rapper], just a lot of that underneath as much as jazz. So it's kind of interesting how those two sisters, the musical genre sisters, are coming together to form this new union in a lot of ways.

JR: [*Nodding thoughtfully*] And I love that people identify the Chicago sound with that kind of fusion. I'm thinking about "Sunday Candy" and it's a gospel-esque progression that Nico wrote." Nico Segal is both a musician and a talented composer credited with producing and collaborating with artists under his own name and formerly as Donnie Trumpet.

Nico writes these chords, and they have both gospel influences, but you also can hear various forms of the improvisational tradition in it and how he approaches playing over it. And then, the way Jamila and Chance sing over it, has you in church, has you certainly in Chicago. It also has you thinking about all of the kinds of musical legacies that they have here. And I love that as you look at the history of the music, history of both jazz and gospel, they come about and have this twin relationship because to your point about sisterhood, they're both coming out of blues and have deep connections to blues, which also of course has deep connections to the Great Migration and what happens when folk come up here and go to Memphis and then come to Chicago and other places, how all of those musical elements are starting to fuse.

And so, when you hear the gospel and you hear jazz and you certainly will therefore be hearing elements of blues. And I love that we today, if we're listening carefully to the past, we'll just naturally bring together these forms of music."

Over the course of the Chicago Overground Showcase, I introduced the audience to about eight acts, mentioning Sun-Ra's days in Chicago, and how seemingly far-out sounds are baked into everyday moments, every strata of Black Chicago. I talked about a recent backyard barbecue I attended, an event graced by my aunt's best friend's mother. The one who dated Sun Ra's bandmate Marshall Allen back in the '50s.

I added that, in Chicago, "future sounds are our birthright, something we feel inextricably tied to. We feel deeply rooted in the past, but you must understand that our past as Black Chicagoans was rooted in the audacity of the belief that we have a future."[11]

When I introduced Ben LaMar Gay, I added that this audacity to believe in a future was despite the threat of death that lurked in the South. "We came to the North not for opportunity, but I'd argue as refugees. Yet, we retain our essential Southernness. . . . And no young artist I know better illustrates all of that more than Ben."

During that same showcase, I introduced the crowd to a young singer named Akenya that I first met when she was still in high school. In my introduction, I asked the audience if they'd ever experienced something that renewed their faith in the miraculous. A few nods. I went on to say that the first time I'd heard Akenya sing at the Harold Washington Branch of the Chicago Public Library ten years prior, I had experienced one of those miracle-affirming moments. Back then, she was performing at an open mic organized by a program called YOUmedia.

As a youth mentor, I was one of the handful of adults allowed in the teens-only space, and I often found it difficult to articulate the truth of what I witnessed there to friends who weren't allowed into it. But I knew, without a doubt, that it was nothing short of astonishing, and that it was a manifestation of the energy I've been tracking my entire adult life.

Often, a key element to the transfer of energy is having a space that's designated (formally or informally) for that transfer. The day I first met Chance the Rapper, I was also at YOUmedia, a space that served that purpose for him, and he literally offered me the shoes off his feet.

Beginning around 2011, I taught a radio production course for teens at a youth program called YOUmedia. Chance was a high school student attending the program.

The program was at the Harold Washington Public Library in downtown Chicago. It was a space where young people could drop in to learn informally about photography, writing, video, and audio. We had a small recording studio, which in a former life was a walk-in closet. We also had an open-mike night called Lyricist Loft, run by our lead instructor, the dynamic Mike Hawkins, who everyone called Brother Mike.

It was teens-only space (outside of instructors and librarians). Back then, I watched the Lyricist Loft sessions every week that I could, certain that I was witnessing something akin to miraculous, iron sharpening iron.

Chance, Noname, Vic Mensa, and Saba are all popular rappers with world renown now, but when I met them they were cool kids, with talent and possibilities still in front of them. Chance was a cool kid. I liked his shoes. Sea-green leather boat shoes.

I told him I liked his shoes. He promptly took them off and picked them up. He held them in front of me. "Do you want them?" he asked, smirking mischievously.

I tell that story not to make him seem immature—just the opposite: I tell that story to tell you that the "black boy joy" that is a part of his public image is real. He was (and is) a bright young person with purpose and hope. The sort of Afro-optimism that permeates so much of the culture of Black Chicago.

He is also a hard worker in the tradition of Chicago musicians who came before him. The year he graduated from Jones College Prep, he announced at the YOUmedia library circulation desk that instead of going straight to college, he was going to focus on his music career. He had recently given me a CD-R copy of *5 Day*, the precursor to his breakthrough mixtape, *10 Day*. *5 Day* was primarily recorded at YOUmedia. He wrote the title on the disc with a black Sharpie in his own hand. I felt trepidation, but Chance followed up by telling us that his father said he'd support him in working toward his goal for a year. I thought to myself, "that's beautiful," and then I thought that I'd just witnessed this young man's work ethic. And if anyone could do it, he could do it.

One evening at the Lyricist Loft open mike, he held the small audience of his fellow teens rapt. He was a compelling performer even then. But he had made a mistake in his performance of his song "Prom Night." He paced the floor. He told the DJ to stop the track.

Most performers know that this is exactly what not to do. What you are supposed to do is soldier through glitches for the sake of the show.

But this wasn't a show. It was a safe place to workshop ideas and hone performance skills.

Brother Mike and I looked at each other knowingly. Brother Mike was a veteran poet, performer, and a skillful educator. He was also a good friend and advocate.

Mike was very close with Chance, and it must be reiterated that much of the young crop of musical talent coming out of Chicago today is a direct result of older artists working with younger artists. Iron sharpening iron.

Chance told the DJ, his close friend Marcus Prince, to play the track again. Prince, known professionally as DJ Such n Such, was a student I worked closely with. He's a trumpet player, and he also coproduced "Prom Night." Chance paced through the song, full of energy. The small crowd even sang the chorus with him: "Any problems, you can call us, / It's all love, it's all love."[12] Chance landed the performance with flying colors, in more ways than one. The song wound up on *10 Day*, and he commenced in passing out mixtapes and building his team for maximum visibility.

A lot has been made of how he hasn't signed a record deal (as of this writing); yet, somehow, Chance is one of the most visible rappers today, having both appeared on *Saturday Night Live* and won Grammy awards. That's because he essentially built an indie record label around himself. Every trapping that a label deal would afford an artist—A&R (artist and repertoire), dope producers, edgy music videos, iconic album cover work, a hype machine, even strong branding—he was able to procure through his relationships with hungry young talents based here in Chicago.

Like ruination in Jamaica, the mass abandonment of record labels that happened in Chicago during the late 1970s and early '80s could look on its face to have been disastrous. And in some ways, it was. A lot of people lost their livelihoods. A number of talented acts fell into obscurity. But, in other ways, the landscape of Chicago remained teeming with life: scrappy house music labels pumped out revolutionary electronic sounds starting in the 1980s, an underground hip-hop community began to develop and thrive not long after, and by 2012, Chance didn't need a record label at all to get his dream off the ground. From my vantage point, the scene today is just as fertile as ever, but like the rest of the recording industry, it looks very different than it did forty years ago.

I knew that Chance's work was paying off one clammy autumn night when I saw him perform at a *10 Day* listening party at LDRS, a hip-hop life-style store that sells luxury casual hats and T-shirts, among other things.

I had never seen him perform outside of the library before, but I was already a fan.

That November night on North Wells Street, LDRS was packed with young fans, and at least one hundred people stood outside in the pouring rain just to see him. This was well before *Acid Rap*, and *10 Day* had not yet been officially released.

I was inside for some of the show but decided that I wanted to be out-side on the rain-slicked asphalt, where the energy was palpable. In that instant, I felt like something important was happening. Something was in the process of being born. Perhaps even reborn.

All of these moments were running through my mind when I was crying in the waiting room at the Stony Island Car Wash. On a small flat screen, they were watching the BET Music Awards, where Chance was receiving a humanitarian award. Not just an award for his great music, but one for his character. I told the older, butter-pecan-colored lady sitting next to me that Chance offered me his shoes once.

VISIONS OF SOUL

AFRO SHEEN, SOUL TRAIN, AND BLACK CHICAGO'S CLOSE-UP

Starting out in media as a radio journalist on Chicago's WVON in the early 1960s, Don Cornelius constructed important relationships with both Chicago music stars and national acts. These relationships would prove invaluable later. When *Soul Train* launched in Chicago in 1970, voiceover work was handled by Joe Cobb (another WVON radio personality), who continued to be "the voice of *Soul Train*" for many years along with another Chicago radio legend: Sid McCoy. Sid McCoy also served as a longtime director on the show. Cobb was the voice that called out "Sooooooooul Train" on each episode. Another Chicago connection: the first *Soul Train* theme song was a funky instrumental titled "Soultrain" by an outfit called the Ramrods, but the song that took viewers to commercial breaks was "Familiar Footsteps," a deep, doo-wop-drenched jam by Chicago's Gene Chandler. An early sponsor was Joe Louis Milk. Joe Louis Milk was originally owned by the legendary Black boxer and was based in Chicago. And *Soul Train*'s ongoing sponsorship by Chicago's Johnson Products (the makers of Afro Sheen and Ultra Sheen) is baked into the very DNA of the show.

Though *Soul Train* hit its funky stride in Los Angeles, its Chicago roots appeared often, especially when guests who were from Chicago got onboard the "hippest trip in America," as Don Cornelius often called it during his lead-ins to the program.

A January 1977 *Soul Train* episode featured Chicago-born-and-bred singer Lou Rawls, who was enjoying a comeback of sorts after some absence from the charts. He performed "You'll Never Find" and "From Now On." Lou was well-known for his "rapping," a smooth style of black vernacular speech. His particular rap was studded with loads of Black Chicago–isms from his "ex-hometown," such as "the hawk," or wintery winds. His interview with Cornelius was steeped in familiarity.

DON CORNELIUS: Okay, we're back with Mr. Lou Rawls, and we were just talking about how long Old Lou has been in the business. [*Pats Lou on the back.*]

LOU RAWLS: Wh- Wait . . . What? [*Both chuckle.*]

DC: That was not what we were talking about . . .

LR: [*Interjects*] No.

DC: We were talking about how long *I've* been in the business . . .

LR: That's right.

DC: Which is a short time compared to a lot of people, right, Lou?

LR: [*Bites lip, feigning consideration.*] That's true, it's short compared to a lot of people in television. But people in radio, gives it . . . it gives it a little more mileage, you know?

DC: I can agree with that.

LR: Actually, what we were really talking about was the fact that the hawk is taking care of business in our ex-hometown . . . is what we really were talking about.

DC: Yes. I was there recently and it was seven . . . above zero . . .

LR: . . . Yeah . . .

DC: [*With false enthusiasm.*] And I just loved it, you know?

LR: [*Dryly*] You did? You know what, man? Imma tell you something . . .

DC: Your face was hurtin', man . . .

LR: Had a permanent smile on, didn'tcha? Permanent grin . . .

DC: Ooh boy.

LR: Every time I hear people say that, "Man I was back home, Jack, and it was sho cool, Jim." . . . Right . . . you got it, baby. The hawk be takin' names, and I ain't playin' with him at all.

DC: I understand you ran into a few of your old friends and they were all inquiring about when you were . . .

LR: [*Interjects*] . . . gonna come back, right.

DC: To Chicago.

LR: They said, "You doin' alright. When you gon come back? You can live on Lake Shore Drive, now!" I said, "that's cool, that's why I ain't comin back, ya dig. Because, I'm doin' alright." Somebody else on this show knows about that, too.

DC: Uh . . .

LR: Your boy.

DC: Young Sid?

LR: Yeah, Young Sid. Right, Yeah. [*Chuckles.*] [Sid McCoy was about fourteen years older than Don, and a veteran of Chicago radio before his stint directing *Soul Train*. He was also the announcer for *Soul Train* for many years.]

DC: The guy we used to listen to on the radio in Chicago.

LR: Right. When we were growing up?

DC: When we were kids?

LR: That's right.

DC: Well, he was just a kid himself.

LR: He was . . .

DC: But, you had to be a grown man to be on the radio. [Sid hosted a late-night jazz show on WCFL starting in the late 1950s.]

LR: That's right, 'cause he was a little bit ahead of us.

DC: We was in grade school . . .

LR: Right.

DC: Cause, you know, he's still my man, 'cause . . .

LR: Hey, I love him, man.

DC: Despite the differential, you know?

LR: I ain't got nothing to do with it. See you gotta deal with it.

DC: No, he directs the show and does an excellent job. I've always idolized him. And the floor director, Joe Henderson is saying that we should move along.

LR: Mmmmhmm. Sid wants us to get off of him, right . . .[1]

An early sponsor of the *Soul Train* was Sears Roebuck & Company. For the first episode, Don Cornelius put up $400 of his own money, but he soon landed the most famous sponsor of *Soul Train*'s thirty-five-year run: Johnson Products, the quintessentially Chicago-based Black business behemoth. The following year, the show's production was moved out to Los Angeles, but an additional program called *Soul Train Local* (hosted by

Clinton Ghent) continued to air on WCIU here in Chicago throughout the 1970s.[2]

Unfortunately, episodes of *Soul Train Local* starring the homegrown talent of Tyrone Davis, The Dells, Curtis Mayfield, Jerry Butler, Gene Chandler, the Chi-Lites, and the Emotions (as well as a number of lesser-known performers like the Sequins) are lost to time, many of them taped over by WCIU . . . repeatedly.

Don Cornelius was more than a television host—he was a producer and an entrepreneur who broadcast visions of Soul (with a capital *S*) to Omaha, Nebraska, Hartford, Connecticut, and all points between. *Soul Train* was the conduit that transmitted the music of lesser-known artists (such as Chicago's own Brighter Side of Darkness) to a much wider audience. Once called a "time capsule" of soul music and culture by Spike Lee, the show also documented beautifully intimate moments with superstars (such as the 1979 appearance of Aretha Franklin, during which she played the piano and sang while encircled by fans). A similar moment with Aretha Franklin (a frequent guest on the show) involved Aretha and Smokey Robinson sitting at the piano, reflecting on their early days in Detroit. They even sang the Miracles' classic "Ooh Baby Baby" together. No band, just two voices and Aretha at the keys. *Soul Train* also documented electrifying live performances (no, not all Soul Train performances were lip-synced) by artists like Sly Stone, James Brown, and Al Green.

Popular Black dances from the Funky Chicken to the Bus Stop to the Roger Rabbit were instantly disseminated from the hood to millions of homes across America.

In short, Don Cornelius was a visionary who created a show unlike any before, or since. It proved that there was an audience for what was once considered an unprofitable niche market. But the ultimate impact of Don Cornelius's creation is that it (and he) made Soul a household name.

Soul Train's improbable rise is one that, in many ways, is an archetypal example of Black radical imagination (laced with afro-optimism) manifested via Black media (though it's not the only example). Chicago was the launching pad for *Ebony/Jet* and, even earlier, the *Chicago Defender*.

Ebony magazine was launched in the 1940s by the Johnson family (no relation to the Johnson Products Johnsons). It was by far the most popular, influential Black magazine of the twentieth century. For decades, the publication served as a family album for Black America. And its rise to prominence was rooted in Black Chicago's spirit of Black radical entrepreneurship and imagination.

＇ ＇ ＇

So it's absolutely natural that *Mahogany*, Diana Ross's cult classic film about a rising fashion design star, is rooted in Chicago.[3] Not only was the film primarily shot in the South Side neighborhoods of Woodlawn and Bronzeville, but the over-the-top tale is alive with imagination, entrepreneurship, sheer improbability, and will that's right at home in Black Chicago.

Diana's character, a design student named Tracy, dreams of a career as a fashion designer. A shop girl at an unnamed fancy department store (clearly Marshall Field's), she spends her evenings sketching and sewing in her apartment, E. Rodney Jones of WVON keeping her company on the radio. One day, she meets an impassioned, community-minded, political candidate played by Billy Dee Williams. They ultimately fall in love and work together to support his campaign. In one notable scene, they stroll down a rubble-strewn street, Black P. Stone Nation spray-painted tags all around them.

Through a series of chance encounters, she becomes the toast of the fashion world—not as a designer, as she dreamed, but as a model and a muse. The glossy, yet bleary-eyed scenes that follow hint at the dark side of the deal she made for fame.

At one point, while staring at the lush grounds of an Italian villa, Tracy declares, "It's a long way from 41st and Ellis"—a long way from her Bronzeville home. Ultimately, she returns to her roots, choosing to return to Chicago for love.

The film is based on a story by a young Jewish woman from the West Coast named Toni Amber.[4]

The Spook Who Sat by the Door is both the antithesis and scrappy older sibling to *Mahogany*.[5] I was sucker-punched by Herbie Hancock's future funk interpretation of a spy/espionage movie score. I was left reeling when I heard the cut that featured a bass guitar overdubbed in reverse. The Chicago roots of the film run deep: from its Chicago setting to where the movie was shot: Gary, Indiana, with a smattering of Chicago shots for credibility.

The roots extend to the man behind the soundtrack: Herbie Hancock was born and raised in Chicago. And Sam Greenlee—one of the screenwriters and the author of the original novel—lived on Chicago's South Side until his death in 2014. The premise of the story is that a social worker turns lone Black CIA agent who goes rogue and ultimately trains a Chicago street gang to be an elite squad of guerrilla warriors dead-set on fighting for a Black revolutionary war in America.

Naturally, in 1960s America, the novel was difficult to get published in the mainstream press. So it's no wonder that (according to Greenlee) although the film took place in the city, the City of Chicago did not okay their request to shoot there. Shots of the 63rd Street El had to be commandeered. Most everything else was shot across the lake in Gary, Indiana, where Richard Hatcher was then that city's first Black mayor. The movie was directed by Ivan Dixon who I know best as the sigh-inducing male lead in the righteous 1964 movie *Nothing but a Man*. He also guest-starred in two episodes of the original *Twilight Zone* that are both worth seeking out. According to entertainment journalist Nina Metz,

> Shortly after it opened in theaters, the film [*The Spook Who Sat by the Door*] vanished altogether—pulled by its distributor, some allege, bowing to pressure from the FBI. The narrative, about disciplined efforts to take down The Man through brain power and armed revolts, was intentionally controversial, and it doesn't take a leap of the imagination to presume the film made those in certain corridors of power nervous enough to "disappear" the movie altogether.
>
> For years it was only available on bootleg video. In 2004, the actor Tim Reid tracked down a remaining negative stored in a vault under a different name ("When they want to lose something, they lose it," Reid told the *Tribune* at the time) and released it on DVD. It still remains largely unknown to the general public, an artifact from the blaxploitation era that defies most of the genre's clichés.[6]

Conversely, *Monkey Hustle* is another film shot Chicago that, at its face, perpetuates many of the genre's stereotypes. But a deeper look at that film reveals much more satisfying metadata.

Monkey Hustle was an American International film that came out in 1976, though it was shot around the same time as 1975's *Cooley High*.[7] Yaphet

Kotto stars as a small-time hustler slash love interest of the lovely Rosalind Cash, who runs a soul food shack called Sweet Mama's. A very young Debbi Morgan was featured as Cash's dimpled daughter. Rudy Ray Moore starred as a flashy neighborhood hero and big-time hustler (who is also Cash's alternate love interest). The other major character is a drummer named Win, Debbi Morgan's love interest. Despite showing promise for bigger things, Win dips deeper and deeper into the "monkey hustle" with Kotto.

Mainly shot around 63rd Street, east of the Dan Ryan Expressway (the Woodlawn neighborhood) and various West Side locations, the film features the city prominently.

A very young Robert Townsend plays Win's bandmate and delivers the memorable line, "Man, up your nose with it!" Robert also had bit parts in *Mahogany* and *Cooley High*.

William Fosser was the film's set decorator. He worked on various plays in Chicago for decades. In the film, the walls of Sweet Mama's illustrate a cross section of Black culture, fittingly featuring posters for Sun Ra and Stanley Turrentine at the New Jazz Showcase, and Festac 77. A poster for Yusef Lateef at the North Park Hotel hangs alongside a sign for homemade ice cream.

In one scene, an LP of the *Sparkle* soundtrack—composed, produced, and recorded by Curtis Mayfield in Chicago—is visible propped up on a shelf.

That soundtrack album, which was originally slated to be recorded by Roberta Flack, wound up being sung by Aretha Franklin, who was able to give Curtis the emotive elements he sought.

By the time the *Sparkle* soundtrack had hit the streets in 1976, Curtis had hit his stride writing and producing a number of successful soundtracks, including 1975's *Let's Do It Again* (with the Staple Singers), 1974's *Claudine* (with Gladys Knight & the Pips), and most famously, his own *Superfly* soundtrack in 1972 (there is a 2018 remake of the film). The film follows the sometimes-harrowing story of a cocaine kingpin named Priest.

In 2017, I asked Todd Mayfield, the second-eldest son of Curtis Mayfield, about a bit of lore surrounding the soundtrack. "The story circulating around . . . says that Curtis was not happy with the themes of the film. That the soundtrack is made to be a very different narrative. And [in Todd's book, *Traveling Soul: The Life of Curtis Mayfield*] you actually gave that story a lot more nuance."[8]

"Right," Todd affirmed. "He just read the script, and . . . his reaction was after seeing the clips in the film was that 'They're doing an awful lot of coke in this movie! Every other scene they're doing some lines of coke.' . . . He said, 'This almost looks like a cocaine commercial.' And he didn't really see that in the script, I guess. It didn't say, 'They do a line of coke here,' or whatever. He had kind of wanted to do a counterweight, a counterbalance to some of those images that were being portrayed in the film. And he really dug deep into what he thought [were] the minds of these characters."

Todd's characterization echoes his father's sentiments, as documented on the 1972 promotional recording titled *Rapping*:

> I really got into the script, the reading of the script . . . the first piece of the movie I had gotten was such a turn-on the way it read.
>
> Actually, to me, it read better than the movie even turned out, because they were able to color it and what have you.[9]

I mentioned to Todd, "There were a lot of people even in that moment, in the Black community, when they saw the movie, they critiqued it because they thought it was blaxploitational. That it was negative, a negative portrayal of Black people."[10]

"Right," he affirmed again.

"But your father, because of his upbringing, where he grew up [the Cabrini Green Housing projects], he had seen people like all of these characters. And so . . . he was sensitive to the . . . humanity of the people. He was able to describe them in the music in ways that still hold up."

Todd nodded. "He said, 'we probably all know a couple of Freddies'—you know, people who may have a drug habit . . . or are just not making the right decisions. You see them walking around all over the place, you know, in the neighborhoods, and maybe even in your own family."

Curtis Mayfield reflected back in 1972 that "Think," an instrumental on the *Superfly* soundtrack, "represented an old gospel feel, and the music itself, and man being black, having a mind, even though [Priest] was involved in such an environment that had him hustling in such manners, he still felt he had to get out. And when Freddie died, and when he saw

Scatter, whom he looked up to all his life, he really had to sort of get into himself, and that was the realization of it."[11]

Monkey Hustle, which was released four years after *Superfly*, was crippled by its share of stereotypical characters, as well. However, the quiet intimacy between Rosalind Cash's Sweet Mama and Yaphet Kotto's Daddy Foxx were surprisingly nuanced, the perfect counter to Yaphet's trickster persona throughout the film.

The movie also captures concrete elements of the community for posterity that are now long gone. There were shots of the Woodlawn Organization's storefront under the Sixty-Third Street El tracks. TWO is a group that has worked to organize and advocate for the Woodlawn community for decades. The stretch of the El that rose above the Woodlawn Organization was razed in 1997. The Exquisite Vogue boutique on 47th Street makes a cameo. And one scene was shot at the now-defunct Skate City at 1234 West 63rd Street (which currently hosts a Missionary Baptist church).

The plot of *Monkey Hustle* is fairly pointed: The city government is pushing ahead on plans to construct an expressway on land currently occupied by the neighborhood (which was actually happening in real-life Chicago ... there were at the time plans for an east-to-west crosstown expressway that never came to fruition). Ultimately the setup becomes that the hustle must go on to save the community (by any means necessary). There's ultimately a tenuous truce to stop the construction of said crosstown Expressway, but even the monkey hustle couldn't stop the so-called urban renewal projects that caused the destruction of the 63rd Street El spur (and much of the commercial development built beneath it). The film ironically serves as scant moving proof of its once-existence. But of course, a short list of mid-1970s films were not the only Chicago visuals being disseminated.

ix

BRAND-NEW YOU

MAKEOVER, MIND OVER

It's notable that both *Ebony/Jet* and *Soul Train* were born in Chicago and that each were Black-produced media entities, not just hollow caricatures of Black people created by people outside of the community.

It's also notable that they each helped shape the collective identity of Black Americans in immeasurable ways. Replicating glowing, aspirational images of Blackness, Black Chicago's mark on the mass media landscape, particularly in the mid-twentieth century, helped fuel the civil rights movement and the overall forward thrust of our people in the twentieth century. The gravity of that task was felt by many of Black Chicago's media creators.

Third World Press publisher and educator Haki Madhubuti wrote in his 1973 book, *From Plan to Planet*, that

> Black writers, as other black creators, deal in images. They understand the uses and manipulation of the image . . .
>
> The responsibility of the black writer is great, greater when put into the context of so few speaking for so many.[1]

He lamented that too many writers and poets didn't take that responsibility seriously enough, and that they thought they were "*stars*": "This is for real. The worldrunners are going to the moon and the 'negroes' are cleaning their Cadillacs and talking about how *bad* they are. But some of us know that, like nations, stars fall everyday."[2] Chicago-based Third World Press is over fifty years old and has published hundreds of influential Black texts by authors including Gwendolyn Brooks, Gil Scott-Heron, Amiri Baraka, Margaret Walker, Sterling Plumpp.

Part of what makes Black Chicago unique from almost any other strain of Black culture is how much control we had at one point over our own image and sound. Our mass media (now almost an antiquated term) had international reach, in some cases became shorthand for American Blackness, and was wholly ours. There is a perception in the age of social media that Black people in the United States are suddenly under siege; that we can scarcely barbecue in a public park, or drive, or wait for friends in a coffee shop while Black. But really, social media is simply delivering to our phones the proof of what's been going on all along.

Back in the day, it was up to Black publications to spread the word of daily indignities and struggles.

Take a 1977 issue of *Jet* with soul group the Emotions smiling on the cover featuring an article noting that a Black family in suburban Chicago was the victim of a cross-burning on their front lawn. The culprits were white youths who later claimed it was a prank. The vandals also smashed the family's living room windows.

Mrs. Katherine Geanes said, "Nobody's going to run us out."[3]

Meaty think pieces bore no hyperlinks and were the domain of Lerone Bennett Jr., or Third World Press, or the *Chicago Defender*'s editorial page, or the barber's chair. In an essay first published in *Ebony* in 1969, Bennett implored:

In a very real sense, the strategy of the rebellion grows out of a situation created and maintained by white Americans. And white Americans will have to make the key revolutionary decision of how much pressure it will take to make them change.[4]

I suppose that hasn't been decided, yet.

And, seldom did the average white American cross paths with most of these platforms. So, in a sense, Black media outlets were early narrowcasters. We could speak among ourselves by the millions.

In 2018, I participated in an Unfurling (essentially a show-and-tell) through the Chicago Public Library and the Art Institute. Sprawled out on a folding table in front of me were some of my old issues of *Ebony*, a few other pieces from Black publications, and recordings from Chicago. Library visitors milled about between exhibitors' tables.

A middle-aged white woman gingerly picked up a 1971 issue of *Ebony* and leafed through it for a long time in silence.

She finally looked up at me and stated, "This is beautiful. I've never picked one of these up before."

Ebony has a dual identity. It is, according to artist Hank Willis Thomas, "the Negro Bible": very literally the written touchstone for Black American imagery and culture in the twentieth century. And to non-Black people, it is often an unknown known (and in some cases, it's completely foreign).

On the flipside, *Soul Train* was a welcome guest in homes across America, regardless of the occupants' color. The show sent positive images of Black people into homes where they might not have otherwise been welcome. The same can also be argued for certain instances of Black radical entrepreneurship that were born here.

I was watching my *Best of "Soul Train"* DVD box set one weekend. The videos include tons of original TV spots for Ultra Sheen and Afro Sheen, and Johnson Products was a primary sponsor of the program. Its hair-care ads showcased a singularly powerful vision of Blackness that perfectly complemented *Soul Train*'s resplendent performances by the likes of the Honey Cone and LTD. They broadcast brief bursts of Black beauty and pride to the nation. And, sometimes, they were even able to slip a bit of Black history in there, too.

In one of Afro Sheen's more memorable television ads from about 1973, a young Black man is admonished by "Frederick Douglass" for his messy afro.

The spot opens with Douglass standing behind the young man who is getting ready for school, books in hand. "Haven't you forgotten something?" Douglass asks the young man.

The young man replies, "Who are . . ." then shouts, "Say, aren't you Fredrick Douglass?"

Douglass nods royally.

BRAND-NEW YOU

"We learned about you in school yesterday. About how you were a slave and how you took your own freedom, and then began to fight for dignity and freedom for all our people. But, what'd I forget?"

"Are you going to go out in the world with your hair like that?"

The young man tries to explain to "Mr. Douglass" that "Times have changed. We wear the natural, now."

Resplendent in a black three-quarter-length coat, bowtie, and jacket, Douglass replies: "You call that a natural? That's a mess. I've been watching the progress of our people, and I'm quite familiar with the natural. And I'm also aware that it's worn as an outward expression of pride and dignity. . . . So, haven't you forgotten . . ."

The young man's eyes light up. "Right," he exclaims, heading toward his dresser. "My Afro Sheen Comb-Easy and hairspray for sheen. You know, I can dig this getting my 'fro together."

The spot ends with a chorus singing the iconic "Beautiful People Use Afro Sheen" tagline, which was crafted in Chicago by the Vince Cullers Advertising Agency—one of the very first Black-owned ad agencies in the country. Known by its Swahili translation, Watu-Wazuri, it's an audacious tagline for an "unapologetically black" brand, fashioned before such a classification existed.

Vince Cullers started his firm in 1956, after growing tired of being turned away from white-only firms. Back then, the idea of a happy Black family on a mainstream ad for margarine was unheard of. Back then, ads for products that weren't specifically for Black people featured happy white people (even in Black publications), because the idea of making ads that catered to the Black demographic was unheard of. Cullers believed that the Black demographic was largely untapped. His firm helped to change the tide with their groundbreaking 1968 contract for Lorillard Inc., the makers of Newport and Kent cigarettes. Cullers's ads, featuring dashiki-clad men and women, captured the moment and proved to be hits. To this day, Newport is considered to be a stereotypically Black cigarette brand.

In the fall of 1969, the first Black Minorites Business and Cultural Expo, or Black Expo, in Chicago distributed a program of events (fig. 9) that includes dozens of ads from local companies that were exhibiting at the expo. Businesses like Gladys' Luncheonette, Ernie Banks Ford, Soul Beauty Cosmetics, and Hop's Black Bag, which features "a progressive new

FIGURE 9. Front and back covers of the 1969 Black Expo program. (Author's personal collection)

approach to men's fashions."[5] Another advertisement is for Vince Cullers Advertising.

The Cullers ad is simple. A plain white background with text in clean, black, san-serif font (fig. 10). The message is clear: the days of the wholesale undervaluing of Black things are through.

So, a couple of years later, Johnson Products' choice of the Black advertising firm, and Cullers's choice to implement a particularly pro-Black message were perfectly in line with their respective track records.

During the glory days of Black hair-care manufacture in Chicago (roughly the 1960s through the 1970s), Johnson Products' annual sales peaked at about $45 million. Built from the ground up out of community need, the company personified archetypal Black radical entrepreneurship.

Black hair care was a field that was entirely ignored by mainstream hair-care product manufacturers for decades. Sure, we had our trusty hot combs and a few go-to pomades, but for the most part, Black folks were often left to our own devices, sometimes concocting hair-raising homebrew straighteners and conditioners, before the explosion of Black-owned hair products beginning in the 1950s. Because the field was virtually untapped by white firms and had a huge potential customer base (at this point, both Black men

113

**blackball,
black book,
black boy,
black eye,
black friday,
black hand,
black heart
blackjack,
black magic,
blackmail,
black market,
black maria,
black mark,
little black sambo.**

white lies.

Black is Beautiful.
Vince Cullers Advertising, Inc.
520 North Michigan Avenue
Chicago, Illinois 60611 (312) 321-9296

FIGURE 10. Vince Cullers Advertising ad in the 1969 Black Expo program. (Author's personal collection)

and women straightened their hair), the first boxed permanent straighteners were the rocket fuel that Black hair-care companies needed to blast off.

During the 1970s, as sales expanded even further, Johnson Products ranked as the largest African American–owned manufacturing company in the nation. In those heady days, alongside Johnson Products, the illustrious Soft Sheen, Supreme Products, and other smaller firms also called the Windy City home. Unfortunately, Johnson Products (the first minority firm to be listed on the American Stock Exchange) was sold to a white firm in 1993, but in 2009 it was acquired by a Black firm based in Dallas.[6]

As with many companies, Johnson Products' path was destined not to remain on an upward trajectory. By 1976, Black cosmetics and hair care accounted for $500 million in sales. And traditionally white companies took note. Beginning in the mid-1970s, the Black hair-care market was raided by the big boys.

Even Revlon began making a relaxer, proudly touting in an ad placed in *Ebony* that "Now You Can Be Beautiful, Too." After the "Black is Beautiful" movement (and the "Beautiful People Use Afro Sheen" tagline), the message that now, because Revlon made a permanent relaxer, Black women can be beautiful "too" was flatly tone deaf. The mainstream cosmetic and toiletry companies that had all but ignored Black consumers were making power plays to woo them. And, sadly, Black-owned Black hair-care companies were the fatalities.

Founder George Johnson saw the writing was on the wall. The company needed to diversify. To expand its consumer base, it began exporting its product to Nigeria in 1974, then Belgium, France, the United Kingdom, and Jamaica. The exports at one point accounted for 10 percent of its sales. But, a simultaneous attempt to stake a flag in the upscale mainstream toiletry market was unsuccessful.

Black Tie was a men's cologne created in 1975 by Johnson Products, which spent liberally to promote it. It even produced a private press LP featuring the ad campaign's jingle (as well as five soulful riffs on the theme, titled "Morning," "Afternoon," "Evening," "Sunset," and "Night"). The campaign aimed to offer consumers a taste of the good life. It was a slice of a dream not unlike the one Johnson had offered everyday Black Chicagoans through romantic Ultra Sheen ads. The TV commercials projected plush imagery, featuring bucolic lawn parties and uptown apartment dwellers.

Unfortunately, that aspirational dream was much more potent to the Black community than to the rest of the general public—particularly coming from Johnson. So, despite the replacement of Black male models with white models, and ad placement in *Time* rather than *Ebony*, the product floundered. And cost Johnson Products dearly.

Late in 1975, however, before the tea leaves could be read on the Black Tie debacle, a *Jet* cover story broke the news about George Johnson's audacious new plan.[7] He was starting an ambitious cosmetology franchise featuring the Ultra Sheen and Afro Sheen family of products. The article was titled "The Prodigal Returns to His First Love: The Beauty Industry," referring to the fact that this attempt to enter the service-based industry of hairdressing (versus the product manufacturing field) was not his first. His foray fifteen years earlier into salon franchising had ended in failure. That was around 1960, long before the breakout success of Afro Sheen and before the firm's long-running, lucrative sponsorship of *Soul Train*.

In the *Jet* article, a photo of Johnson in his handsome, modern, wood-paneled office bore the accompanying caption: "Working as a cosmetics production chemist and moonlighting as a busboy, Johnson began climb to success."[8]

That brief caption captures what fuels Black Chicago's ever-expanding network of hustles: stories that stoke belief in the improbable and faith in fruits of self-determination. That network, which spanned the spectrum of business ventures, helped make Chicago an attractive place for a young Oprah Winfrey not only to lay down roots but to begin to build her media empire. A reputation steadily built on entrepreneurs and journeymen.

A common earmark of Black Chicago hustle is the utilization of collective power through shared economics. Another way to describe this notion is through a now-antiquated phrase known as nation building. At the most literal level, nation building occurs through the creation of new Black life, a child who is then raised up to be an asset to the community. A secondary—but crucial—form of nation building is the construction of strong Black autonomous economies. In the *Jet* article, Johnson exemplifies that tenet.

Johnson's franchises were to be called Ultra Sheen Beauty Boutiques. He said he was aiming to "pick up Madame Walker's dream of an organized industry."[9]

He clarified his intent further. "I offer this program not only so that we, the participants, can achieve comfortable profits and income, but so that we can begin to develop a solid economic base within the Black community. In this way, the profits will remain in the Black community for reinvestment and recycling."[10] Through the franchises, Johnson projected the creation of 42,000 new jobs in the Black community.

Jet ran a modest follow-up piece in April 1977 announcing that the first Ultra Sheen Beauty Boutique would open in Chicago that month.[11] The actual opening was delayed until June. According to a *Jet* brief, it was to be managed by Johnson's daughter-in-Law, Renee, and his son, Eric. It noted that the South Side boutique offered "complete body care."[12] The franchising never took off, perhaps due to poor timing. The first Ultra Sheen Beauty Boutique had launched just as Johnson Products, the first majority-Black-owned company on the American Stock Exchange, was beginning to falter.

Then in 1980, in an effort to combat lower overall sales, Johnson Products set up a West African Division in Lagos, Nigeria. But, due to a change in Nigerian trade law, the company had to import all of its chemicals and other materials used to manufacture its products in Nigeria, which made products considerably more expensive there than they were in the United States.[13]

Johnson was quickly crippled by smugglers who purchased U.S.-produced jars of Ultra Sheen and sold them in Nigeria cheaper than Johnson Products could afford to sell its own African-manufactured goods. When Johnson sold a jar of hair relaxer for twenty dollars, smugglers undercut them at eighteen. Then Johnson dropped the price to sixteen dollars, and smugglers dropped theirs to fourteen. According to Marilyn Cason, the director of Johnson's Nigerian division in 1982, "The lowest price the smuggler could ask for hair relaxer and still make a profit was $4.60 a jar. So we dropped our price to $4.50."[14] The operation bled money.

By 1993, Johnson Products had slipped to second in the hierarchy of the Black care products market. First place at the time was Soft Sheen, also out of Chicago. Despite the slip, Johnson Products was still one of the largest Black-owned firms in the country, but an ominous sign was three leadership changes in four years, following the divorce of George and Joan Johnson.[15]

George's son Eric (who had run the Soft Sheen Beauty Boutique with his wife, Renee), was chief executive of Johnson Products when the company accepted a buyout from a Miami-based corporation. About ten years later, the company was sold to Procter & Gamble. Then, as already mentioned, it was purchased in 2009 by a group of Black investors with the goal of returning the company to Black hands, but in today's very hot Black hair-care field, Ultra Sheen has yet to see a return to the crown, so to speak.

The 1993 Johnson Products buyout was a warning shot, signaling that the behemoth had fallen, and that the era of mighty Black-owned hair-care companies was coming to an end.

Meanwhile, "Soft Sheen, which had about 400 employees in the Chicago area and $100 million in annual sales by the mid-1990s, was sold in 1998 to French company L'Oréal," and a fairly new manufacturing plant on 87th Street was shuttered soon after.[16] The company's headquarters were shifted elsewhere.[17] It's a starkly contradictory message from the one that Ed Garner's success sent to Black Chicagoans. The message that whispered that "*you, too, can live in a place like the brick Soft Sheen Mansion*," nestled in the Black middle-class enclave of West Chesterfield.

But, back in 1982, Soft Sheen was still riding high, and Sheila Hutchinson (then recording as Sheila Hutchinson-Whitt), the lead vocalist from the Emotions (also from Chicago), sang a Soft Sheen radio jingle called "New You in '82." The song sounds like some joyful lost Emotions or, perhaps, like an Earth, Wind & Fire number. The upbeat, empowering jingle was written by a team that included Chuck Colbert (once a member of The American Breed, and a founding member of the funk band Rufus), and was produced by a South Side firm called ECO (Ethnic Communications Outlet).

Make over
Bring out the best in you!
Shape over
Get your body together, too![18]

"New You in '82" became the theme for a Soft Sheen–produced, five-minute segment that aired on WJPC, a now-defunct soul radio station owned by *Ebony/Jet* and housed in the Johnson Publishing Building. The segment promoted healthy living, "Mind, Body, and Soul." And according to *Jet*, the project encompassed "three basic themes; Make-Over/Looking

Good, Shape-Over/Feeling good and Mind-Over Everything/Thinking Good."[19]

Soft Sheen's then-president Ed Gardner noted that in addition to making quality products the company's concern was "also to help improve the quality of life for the community as well."[20] Guests on the segment included Dr. Alvenia Fulton, nutritionist and owner of South Side health food emporium Fultonia.

Born in 1906, Alvenia was introduced to herbal medicine by her parents while growing up in Middle, Tennessee.[21] She later earned a degree in naturopathic medicine from the Lincoln College of Naturopathy, and also graduated from Greater Payne Theological Seminary. Fulton's adherences to religion and natural healing methods were unwavering: she consulted God before making her herbal healing compounds. She also deeply believed in the healing power of food.

Beginning in the 1950s, she operated the Fultonia Health Food Center (later the Fultonia Health and Fasting Institute), which was at one time located at 521 East 63rd Street (later at 1953 West 63rd Street), as well as the Ancient Baking Co. at 6308 South Rhodes (fig. 11). She was also an author, publishing books such as *The Fasting Primer* and *The Nutrition Bible*.

Fulton was a natural healing pioneer and is credited with teaching entertainer and activist Dick Gregory about eating a meatless diet (among many, many, others who learned under her tutelage).

She lived to be ninety-two years old, outliving many of her detractors.

The recording that I have of the "New You" jingle—all that's left of that WJPC segment—makes me feel like I'm ready to face 1982 (or just about anything else, for that matter), too. But who knew in 1982 what was to come for the house that the Gardners built?

The lovely Soft Sheen factory campus that Ed Gardner built from scratch at 87th Street and the Dan Ryan Expressway had lain fallow for the two decades since the company was sold to L'Oréal. Evergreens were uprooted and the flagpole stood bare. In 2019, a sign was erected on the campus announcing plans to convert it into a charter school.

But in 2012, while the fate of the campus was still uncertain, the multimillionaire Ed Gardner staged a protest to insist that a planned shopping development in a Black area hire more Black construction workers. At that time he was over eighty years old and had long since sold Soft Sheen, but he

DEAR MRS. FULTON:

As I prepare to produce The Passion Play for the 40th time, I cannot help but pause to say thank you once again for restoring my health. You know better than most that I was as close to death as I could get when I came to you in August of 1963 for help. Five weeks later, I rented Arie Crown Theater in McCormick Place to produce The Passion Play again for the first time in five years. Through your counsel, your knowledge for the magic of food, and your loving care, I made a miraculous recovery. Since then I have eaten health foods with your constant attention to my diet and I have never felt better in all of my life.

If it had not been for you, there would have been no Passion Play in 1964, 1965, 1966, nor would I be producing The Passion Play tonight. God Bless You.

With deep gratitude,
WILLA SAUNDERS JONES

Fultonia Health Food Center

Visit our beautiful Tropical Setting
521 EAST 63rd STREET — 684-5700

MRS. ALVENIA F. FULTON,
Nutritionist, Food Consultant

Ancient Baking Co.

Bring us your diet problems. Keep your health up and your weight down.
"Your Health and Diet needs our SPECIALTY"
using the finest natural and organic ingredients

Special in diabetic foods, salt free foods, allergy foods, special diet foods, sugar free and low calorie foods.
Health Foods - Cakes - Pies- Cookies - Breads - Rolls

We follow your doctor's diet specifications

OPEN DAILY 12 NOON — 8:00 P.M.
6308 SOUTH RHODES AVENUE   684-5700

Subsidiary of FULTONIA HEALTH FOODS CENTER
521 EAST 63rd STREET   684-5700
Chicago, Illinois 60637

FIGURE 11. Fultonia advertisement from 1969 Black Expo program. (Author's personal collection)

still felt the need to wield his power. This effort was in line with Operation Breadbasket initiatives in the 1960s and early 1970s that were designed to stop the discriminatory business practices limiting economic parity between Blacks and whites. Though seen as heroic at the time, little has changed since Garner's 2012 activism about construction hiring practices in Chicago.

LaCade makes the most of your hair

And soft, touchable hair makes life more beautiful. More fun to share. Whatever you've done to hurt your hair . . . over-permed or pressed. LaCade hair care products restore naturally healthy shine and softness. Even help hair repair itself. Check into these rich natural hair care products. For traveling in beautiful style, LaCade hair care makes it!

If not available at your favorite store use this coupon

Mail to:

La Cade
PRODUCTS COMPANY

2401 S. Michigan Av.
Chicago, Ill. 60616

Guaranteed

©1974 LaCade
Products Company

Please send me: (write quantity of each item in box)
All of these LA CADE Hair Care Products are rich in Hormones and Vitamins A & D:

☐ HORMONE HAIR GROWTH TREATMENT . . with Protein and natural estrogenic substances. Specifically aids weak, thinning hair. 2 oz. $2.50.   4 oz. $4.50.
☐ HORMONE SHAMPOO . . with vitamins A & D and more Protein than other shampoos. Biodegradable. 4 oz. $1.50
☐ CONDITIONER & RINSE . . Moisturizing protein conditioner. No tangles, no frizz. 4 oz. $2.25
☐ ULTRA MINK HAIR DRESSING & SCALP CONDITIONER . . with genuine Mink Oil—not a drop of water. 2 oz. $1.50   8 oz. $3.50
☐ BREAK NO MORE . . Clinically proven hair repair. Stops breakage. Saves naturals. 4 oz. $2.95
☐ HORMONE PRESSING CREME . . . New! World's first pressing creme with hormones. Protects hair. 3 oz. $1.50

TOTAL AMOUNT $_____
(add 75¢ for postage & handling. Check or Money Order only. No C.O.D. please)

Name:_____
Address_____
City_____State_____Zip_____

Name of Store
you usually shop at:_____

FIGURE 12. La Cade advertisement in *Ebony* (September 1974, p. 86). (Author's personal collection)

La Cade Products was another of many Chicago-based Black hair-care firms during the late 1960s through the '70s. Though not as well-known as Supreme Products (producers of Duke and Raveen) or Johnson Products (producers of Afro Sheen and Ultra Sheen), La Cade left behind scant but fascinating evidence of its existence. First off, it left some pretty great advertisements starting around 1972 (my favorite is figure 12, from a 1974 *Ebony* issue). How's that for swagger?

There's a sort of street-romantic, cinematic appeal to the image in the ad. A lovely Black man with a thick mustache and wide-brimmed hat, clutched by a windswept, breathless woman.

La Cade also came up with some clever product names (one of which got the company in legal trouble, as I delve into later). Most notably, to me is that sometime around 1974 La Cade decided to put together a small recording division, based at its corporate headquarters (2411 South Michigan in Chicago). They recorded two artists on two singles, both of which are as gritty and charismatic as the ad in figure 12. The first is "The Beginning of the Void," the B-side of "Love Me Too" by Danny Hunt (who sounds to me very much like a young Stevie Wonder on his records). I love this record. Very soulful, with a stone-cold groove, the lyrics are acutely socially aware and include these lines: "Just another ghetto child / never seen his Daddy smile / He's in the beginning of his void."[22]

The following year, Hunt released a beast of a cut arranged by the iconic Tom Tom Washington and released on Dynamite Records (another tiny Chicago-based imprint). As of this writing, Danny Hunt is alive and well in the Chicago area and singing gospel music.

The other record I have found is by Walter "Butterball" Davis, titled "Baby (Wacha Doin' to Me)" backed by "Girl Stop Begging." He had also put out a record called "Nobody Cares for a Junkie" on Butterball Records . . . it's deep. Really deep. But, back to "Girl Stop Begging": the cut is a bluesy-funky little gem penned by Davis himself.

Both records suffered from lack of promotion and distribution and stalled out. It was about this time that La Cade trademarked a product name that I think is very 1970s and cool: "The Last Tangle," presumably inspired by the controversial 1972 film *Last Tango in Paris*. In the film (which was rated X at the time but is now "NC-17," whatever that means), Marlon Brando's middle-aged character has a torrid affair with a soon-to-be-married young Parisian woman with scandalous results. Oh yes, these La Cade folks had some swagger. Not long after La Cade's foray into the record business, it was embroiled in a legal battle with Roux Laboratories over a product name. Roux initially contested La Cade's claim to copyright the term "Mink" in La Cade's Ultra Mink product. With a hair product called White Minx on the market, Roux complained that the product names were too similar. The case took a turn in 1977 when Roux's counsel came forward with this gem of an argument during the proceedings:

> I would like to renew my running objection that the only question involved here is the applicant's right to use the descriptive term "ultra."
>
> We do not object to its use of the term "Mink," which has been disclaimed by applicant. Neither have we objected to the use of others using the term "Mink," but we are objecting to the use of the descriptive term "ultra" which we had adopted and used as part of the "ultra White Minx" trademark but using "ultra" merely in its descriptive connotation, and that is the whole substance of this opposition.[23]

That nonsense pretty much spelled the end of the case for Roux. Ultimately, it dropped the complaint, but not before costing La Cade a lot of money in legal fees. By 1977, the firm had stopped advertising in *Ebony*, had stopped releasing records, and the trail goes otherwise cold. But, in a few short years, La Cade surely left behind some waves: both soundwaves and hair waves.

All this is not to say that there are no Black hair-care companies left in Chicago. Today, the Black hair-care legacy continues through companies like Luster Products (founded by Fred Luster Sr. in 1957), which is still based in Chicago. Luster, home of the ubiquitous Pink products (e.g., Pink Lotion), spearheaded AHBAI, a collective of Black-owned hair-care companies that formed in 1981 and created the Proud Lady logo (a braided woman in profile); the group publicized that even in the 1980s, a period of continued upheaval and consolidation in the industry, many hair-care businesses were Black-owned.

Luster Products is still owned and operated by the Luster family.

In 2017, Jory Luster (president of Luster Products) was quoted as saying, "Our customers celebrate themselves. We can be beautiful with what God gave us. We are proud of ourselves, our looks, and our heritage."[24]

＊　＊　＊

Another small business that begat record labels was Barney's Records. A Black record store with a Black record label made perfect sense in the era when music came pressed on black wax. Barney's Records was on the West Side, at 3234 West Roosevelt Road in Lawndale. Lawndale was the neighborhood where, in 1966, Martin Luther King Jr. lived in a dilapidated building to fight for open housing. One label, Four Brothers, ran from 1965 through 1967; Bright Star was its sister label.

The stakeholders were Willie Barney, Jack Daniels (who served as an A&R/production man), and Granville White. the Four Brothers name referred to Barney's four sons.[25]

Along with singer-songwriter Johnny Moore, Jack Daniels cut a number of hard-hitting soul records during this period on other local labels like Blue Rock and Mercury. The music on Four Brothers followed suit, a perfect union of soul and gritty electrified blues. The first release, Four Brothers 400, was credited to Sam & Kitty: "Don't Hit on Me" backed with "Your Money—My Love." The second, Four Brothers 401 was by Ricky Allen, "I Can't Stand No Signifying" backed with "I'm a Real Thankful Man."

Ricky Allen had a local hit with "You Better Be Sure" and in 1963, his hit "Cut You A-Loose" reached number 20 in *Billboard*'s R&B chart. His recordings from the 1960s—such as "It's a Mess I Tell You," which came out on one of Barney's-connected labels—are perfect soul-blues meldings.

Decades later, one of the four brothers, Ray Barney, followed in his father's footsteps and ran a legendary house music record label called Dance Mania, which he ran and distributed through Barney's Records.

＊　＊　＊

Black-owned businesses like La Cade, Barney's Record Shop, and Soft Sheen are economic engines for communities. And, in Chicago historically, Black-owned businesses practiced a form of Black radical entrepreneurship. They served as economic engines for the civil rights and Black Power movements in Chicago, as well.

The term "civil rights movement" often conjures images of the Deep South, but Chicago was a key battleground in the 1960s and 1970s. This was so not just because of the influx of new Black citizens that the Great Migration delivered, but because of the ongoing struggles for housing equality and empowerment exacerbated by said influx.

Jesse Jackson, whose ties to Dr. King traced back to the campaign at Selma in 1965, was selected by King to head Operation Breadbasket's

Chicago branch. True to its name, Operation Breadbasket distributed nourishment to the community, but it also played a more proactive role to fighting for social justice.

Tactics such as boycotts were implemented, but according to authors David T. Beito and Linda Royster Beito, a seamier aspect including cronyism and strong-arming businesses to donate money to Operation Breadbasket were folded into the tactics, as well.[26]

Eventually, leadership rifts came to a head, and in December 1971, Jackson fell out with Ralph Abernathy, King's successor as head of the national SCLC. Jackson and his allies broke off and formed Operation PUSH (People United to Save Humanity).[27]

This was a pivotal moment in Chicago history because a giant, organized Black party (the largest in Chicago at the time) broke off into factions and never regained the traction it had built before that point. Then, in the subsequent decade, crack cocaine hit the community like an atomic bomb—and the fallout from that explosion is still being felt.

It's clear that the strength of the expo era was rooted on the momentum created in the preceding years, in conjunction with the genius of marketing with a major motion picture (more of this below) and tons of press. Documentation equals existence itself, and media has the power to romanticize just about anything.

About the 1971 expo, *Time* noted: "When the five-day trade fair opened in Chicago last week, there were representatives of nearly 400 black firms on hand to prove the premise. But before the week was out, Black Expo proved to be more than a display of the products of America's fledgling black capitalism. It turned out to be an unofficial convention of entrepreneurs and politicians in search of power at the polls as well as in the marketplace."[28]

Wow. There was even a documentary based on one year's theme: *Save the Children*.[29]

This was a moment ripe with possibilities.

Black businessmen from 40 states gave their backing to Jackson's assertion that economic development—"green power"—is the way to black power. Self-sufficiency, Jackson said during the opening-day ceremonies, "is the first step in breaking out of the ghetto." Said Jackson: "We do not want a welfare state. We have potential. We can produce. We can feed ourselves." Despite the enthusiastic speeches, however, black capitalism is still in an initial stage of development. Aware of that, Jackson proposed a "domestic Marshall Plan" to help black neighborhoods develop their economic potential.[30]

So what happened?

Twenty years later, Ray Quintanilla wrote about Black Expo in the *Chicago Reporter*:

> When about 250,000 people, most of them African Americans, turned out for this year's Chicago Black Expo, many were offered fried chicken and menthol cigarettes . . .
>
> . . . But there are signs of trouble brewing for Black Expo. Some small-business experts and black entrepreneurs say such expositions don't spur actual black business development. Others complain that corporate sponsors are promoting products, such as alcohol and tobacco, that are harmful. And they say that cultural enrichment has taken a back seat to profits.[31]

In the end, please leave me the romance. Let me believe that we were *so* close to breaking free. It gives me a whispered myth to build tomorrow on.

THE COILING FEEDBACK LOOP OF TIME

In the spring of 2016, on the whitewashed belly of a train overpass, someone scrawled "yo pharoah" in royal-blue spray paint. It happened on 75th Street.

The tag appeared again a month or so later on another decayed concrete wall. Urban hieroglyphics. But how to decipher it?

It could be read as "yo" or "your" pharaoh. A term of endearment. How sweet.

Or, it could be read as "yo" as in "hey" pharaoh. Calling out to an unseen street monarch.

Staring absentmindedly at the royal-blue block letters at 75th Street and South Chicago Avenue, I thought of the Affro-Arts Theater, run by Phil Cohran at 3847 South Drexel. In addition to music, the space presented lessons in Swahili and Arabic, as well as cultural history presentations.[1] Among many Black creatives who flocked to the theater were a teenaged Chaka Khan (before her days in Rufus) and her sister, Taka Boom. The constellation of musicians collected around him at the time, called the African Heritage Ensemble, became known as the Pharaohs. That group evolved into Earth, Wind & Fire, but not before releasing one album.

Affro-Arts was closed by the city more than once for various infractions. It had a tumultuous relationship with the police. At one point, the marquee bore the message "closed by deceit." The space was closed four days after Stokely Carmichael spoke there in March 1968.[2] The space reopened in the wake of Dr. King's assassination in April. The *Tribune* chronicled a subsequent reclosing in May, followed by a reopening, still without proper licensing, in July, after Columbia College Chicago held a conference on arts and the inner city. An adviser to then-mayor Richard J. Daley recommended that the theater be reopened.

November 2013. Eating roast-duck wonton soup and sipping red tea at a Hong Kong–style barbecue in Uptown. I verbalize to my companions the change I feel is brewing.

There's a lot of discussion in creative circles about the transfer of community from being a mostly physical space to being a digital one. I think that here in Chicago, young Black artists are (returning to) recognizing the need for shared physical spaces that we have control over. That last part, the "that we have control over" part, is key. We can all feel as though we have an ownership stake in someone else's thing, but ultimately the thing we are building is not ours. In the case of a messy divorce, that point will be made clear.

Watching Josephine Baker's final film, *Princess Tam Tam* (1935), I was reminded of myriad ideas.

She is, in the film, a roman candle. She is the lifeblood of what is built around her. Pure energy and talent. But everything must first pass though filters of respectability and the European gaze. In the film, she eventually opts out of the whole system.

Two phrases really get to the meat of this issue: arts infrastructure and arts stakeholders.

In recent years, young Black creative people have been moving to Chicago (often to attend art school), and young Chicago-bred artists (especially musicians) are choosing to stay, even while Black Chicago as a whole is depopulating. If physical space is no longer important, if community is no longer concrete, why is this even important?

By 2015, Theaster Gates had begun to speak publicly of the importance of Black space. To tease that out a bit more, I'd add the clarifying words "curated" or even "owned." We'd had enough of Black culture being used as currency in conversations that rarely included us. We'd had enough of seeing our art shipped off and stripped of its context for others' revision and consumption.

In a moment after Johnson Publishing sold its publications to an equity firm, and its Michigan Avenue high rise lay dormant, the phrase "Black Curated" had a particular bit of relevance.

Ebony was initially patterned after *Life* magazine (a now-defunct, groundbreaking, large-format photojournalism magazine). In fact, its iconic red rectangular "EBONY" logo with sans-serif block white lettering was nearly identical to *Life*'s logo.

As the publication grew, its dedication to photojournalism remained a core focus. At its peak, *Ebony* was home to Pulitzer Prize–winning photographer Moneta Sleet Jr., among other giants in the field. By the twenty-first century, however, *Ebony*'s popularity (along with the popularity of print magazines in general) had waned. Still, its impact on Black representation and even identity has been incalculable.

Eunice Johnson (1916–2010), widow of *Ebony/Jet* publisher John H. Johnson, was more than Black media's First Lady. As creator and director of the Ebony Fashion Fair (an all-Black roadshow of haute couture), she paved the way for generations of Black models from Beverly Johnson and Naomi Sims to Naomi Campbell. In fact, Richard Roundtree ("Shaft") was a Fashion Fair model before he was kicking tail on the big screen. In the show, which was started in 1961, she included some of the most fashion-forward designers, including Yves Saint Laurent, who Mrs. Johnson had a particularly close working relationship with. In a time when Chicago was in many ways the hub of culture and information that bound the Black community together (e.g., the nationally recognized *Chicago Defender*, *Ebony*, *Jet*, and a world-renowned music and arts scene), Mrs. Johnson took her fashion crusade to the streets in towns both near and remote. Accordingly, sewing machines buzzed each season, inspired by the roadshow of dreams.

When the roadshow began, Blacks were not even welcome in many of the department stores that carried high-end fashions. And Black models had not made it to mainstream catwalks.

Her shows, as well as so many of those classic *Ebony* magazine fashion layouts, presented our people as we were (and still are) striving to be:

free and uplifted. Strutting. Gliding. As if that weren't enough, Ebony Fashion Fair, which grew into the world's largest traveling fashion show, annually encompasses a nearly 180-city tour of the United States, Canada, and the Caribbean. It has raised more than $55 million for various charities. And it kept us dreaming. To me, that is Eunice Johnson's legacy. She brought the dream to our door. Not long after her death, the Ebony Fashion Fair archive of clothing was auctioned off. The roadshow was shut down. This proved to be only the first of many sales of Ebony/Jet's physical assets.

In 2010, Ebony digitized its archives and made the results searchable for free via Google Books. Something to celebrate. Ebony was the premier photojournalism and news magazine of the Black Diaspora for decades. During its peak, Ebony featured groundbreaking work by photographers such as Gordon Parks, as well as thought-provoking articles that exposed sometimes obscure corners of the "Black experience" (mixed-race children of World War II GIs in Japan, Black scuba divers, Black opera singers, et al.). A beautiful thing. A contender has yet to truly pick up that mantle.

The following year, the magazine donated the physical contents of its research library (which included a bound archive of its publications) to artist Theaster Gates.

By 2010, it sold well under expectations and was in need of an aesthetic revamp. There was talk of selling the magazine. But, first the firm gave it another shot. Its first move was to bring in Desiree Rogers as CEO. Then Amy DuBois Barnett (of Honey magazine, sadly shuttered circa 2006) was hired as editor followed by young, fresh talent from Vanity Fair and a slew of other sources. Next, the team commenced in the first full overhaul of the magazine since 1945. The first revamped Ebony appeared in April 2011. That year, the editorial staff captured cutting-edge yet approachable Black culture, art, music, and thought. Features covered topics as varied as the then-recent retrospective of Black visual artist Glenn Ligon, underground soul vocalist Jesse Boykins III, what Black fashion bloggers were wearing during New York's Fashion Week (hint: it was fly), and cultural critic Touré unpacking the rhetoric of "post-Blackness." The full tonal spectrum of Black beauty appeared in the fashion/beauty sections, something that had been slipping a bit in recent years. In short, they worked it out. It showed. By the summer of 2011, Ebony's annual circulation averaged 1,235,865 (a

10.9 percent increase from January of that year), and *Jet*'s grew to 820,557 (a 7.6 percent increase over the same time period).

The following year, Johnson Publishing sold its building. That "Black space" sat dormant, awaiting its next phase. Soon after, Amy DuBois Barnett was out.

Then, Johnson Publishing ceased physical publication of *Jet*. Though tiny, *Jet* was deeply important: many goings-on in Black America were noted only in *Jet*. From the celebratory to the grave . . . the mundane to the fantastical; *Jet* saved hundreds of thousands of Black happenings from obscurity with its net of clever blurbs. *Jet* was also the conduit that turned an image of Mamie Till-Bradley's son Emmett into a rallying cry for the civil rights movement. Mainstream publications had refused to publish images of his mangled corpse.

In addition to being the leading national source of hard Black news for decades, *Jet* also highlighted innumerable lighter moments of Black life, with a particular eye for Chicago. This was partly due to proximity, and partly due to the facts that Chicago was the second-largest city in the country for most of the twentieth century and it has a very large Black population. This is from a 1973 *Jet* society blurb:

> Mrs. Helen Maybell, owner of Soul Queen Restaurant in Chicago, models a fashionable gown after she wins the National Best Dressed Church Women's Award recently during the presentation of the Hall of Fame For Black Designers held in Chicago. Mrs. Maybell's gown, designed by Hanae Mori from Japan, was purchased from the EBONY Fashion Fair collection.[3]

In the accompanying black-and-white photo, Ms. Maybell strolls a catwalk, head uplifted, in a chiffon confection of an unknown hue. What a vignette.

A seventy-odd-year-old publication of record for Black America was gone. And, as we'd find out, *Ebony* was on life support.

Then came word that Johnson Publishing sold an ownership stake in *Ebony* to a group of investors in Texas. This was followed by the announcement that Johnson Publishing was looking for a bidder for its epic photo archive. There is no singular source in the world with as expansive and complete an image resource documenting the civil rights movement and beyond. The archive is our Black Getty Images. But on a more intimate level, it was as though someone was putting Black America's family photo album up for sale. Perhaps fittingly (or perhaps ironically), the photo archive was ultimately sold to a conglomerate of foundations in concert with the J. Paul Getty Trust.

Then the shocker: in 2017, Johnson Publishing announced that it was moving its home base to Los Angeles. The move seemed to follow the publication's trajectory toward a focus on entertainment news. But, to reiterate, the magazine had not been doing well on that path. *Ebony* quietly ceased print publication in the spring of 2019, and the publishers were forced into bankruptcy in 2020. The magazine was sold in bankruptcy court to businessman and former NBA player Ulysses "Junior" Bridgeman.

In the years leading up to bankruptcy, it was unclear what the editorial priority of *Ebony* was, outside of basic survival. The product seemed to simply attempt to follow pace with the news cycle, relying primarily on celebrity updates. Web stories included "Lala Anthony Isn't Rushing to Divorce Carmelo Anthony," recounting an interview with Lala on *The Wendy Williams Show* that day.[4] They lacked a definitive voice, as well as the Black radical imagination and Afro-optimism so imbued into the brand's heritage. *Ebony*'s decisions seemed reactionary, which was the opposite of what the Johnsons worked so hard for.

And, to date, no one has taken the reins as Black America's publication of record for heavier news. That space in media is wide open. And in a moment when Black Lives Matter and all manner of inequalities are on the top of many people's minds, a retooled *Ebony* could certainly retake the throne it built. But what's to come for the storied publication remains to be seen.

Meanwhile, the Ebony/Jet building sat idle for nearly a decade, like so many South and West Side bungalows formerly occupied by families but now boarded-up and forlorn. Except this eleven-story building had the remnants of a radio station, cafeteria, in-house library, and an endless array of implausibly beautiful mid-century modern accoutrements.

The official story behind the sale of the building was that the magazine industry had changed. The building was custom-built for a very specific Johnson Publishing. That company had gone from hundreds of employees down to about thirty-five. There was no reason to hang on to the building.

My hope was that *Ebony/Jet* would form a nonprofit foundation and set up unused portions of the building as a museum and library of Black culture, complete with the cafeteria retooled as a restaurant. The radio station could have served as a space for Johnson Publishing to produce podcasts, one of a few spaces of growth in Black media. Even without expensive recording equipment, the studio buildout would be expensive to replicate elsewhere. They could have rented out meeting and event spaces (the reception floor can accommodate a thousand people). Films could be screened in the theater. They could have even set up a little gift shop with *Ebony*- and *Jet*-branded gear.

Johnson Publishing already had collections that museums today could never replicate: of fashion, photography, books, and a fairly extensive collection of Black art by the likes of Hale Woodruff, Eldzier Cortor, Margaret Burroughs, Romare Bearden, and Richard Hunt.[5] The fashion alone is part of a successful traveling museum exhibition called "Inspiring Beauty: Fifty Years of Ebony Fashion Fair" curated by Joy Bivins, who at the time was at the Chicago History Museum. "Inspiring Beauty" had been touring since 2013, halted only by the Covid-19 pandemic.

I was inside the Ebony/Jet building during its last year as a functioning magazine headquarters, and I can vouch that a museum/library would have been unbelievable. And the building's location downtown in the mix of Michigan Avenue is incomparable.

But instead, it was decided that, in order to move forward, Johnson Publishing needed to shed its assets. Which is the supreme shame in all of this.

The buyers of the building, Columbia College Chicago, hit some hard times of its own not long after the purchase. The word was that Columbia could scarcely afford to properly heat the building, let alone remodel it as planned (which is perhaps for the best, because much of the interior design and architecture survived longer than they would have otherwise, even though the assets have been disseminated). The building ultimately become condominiums, rebranded as 820 South Michigan, bearing scarcely a trace of its midcentury-era splendor.

I say this not to be nostalgic. Then was then. But what we as a people need now is not so different than what we needed then, both nationally and in Chicago.

In Chicago, the post–civil rights era was a renaissance of Black business and Black arts. Today, Black arts circles aim to rejuvenate the economy of the South Side, and to increase spaces for creative endeavors.

For instance, entrepreneur Bernard Loyd bought the Forum in Bronzeville, a long-shuttered dance hall and commercial space and has been working for years to restore it to its earlier glory. In the meantime, he's spearheaded a weekly seasonal marketplace in the Washington Park neighborhood created out of repurposed shipping containers (or boxcars) called Boxville. It's situated in a vacant lot near the 51st Street Green Line El station.

Alternately, artist Faheem Majeed has worked for years to "create platforms" for other artists outside the walls of traditional arts institutions. He is a codirector of an ongoing project—the Floating Museum, which literally floated down the Chicago River on a concrete barge during the summer of 2017. He presented visual arts, including a huge, bright-yellow bust of Jean Baptiste DuSable that eventually found a home at DuSable Park near Navy Pier. He also programmed performances by artists like dancer Vershawn Sanders Ward and the band avery r. young and de deacon board. I also deejayed on the barge, which gave me a unique vantage point of how passersby on Chicago's Riverwalk interacted with the museum. Faheem told me that he wanted to create a platform that broke down the walls of traditional museums that are often exclusionary by design.[6]

But Floating Museum was not Faheem's first dance. Back in 2013, the platform he created was called Shacks and Shanties.

On Chicago's South Side, small wooden shacks more likely serve as newspaper stands or doghouses than as places to present art. Meanwhile, the South Side has a deep shortage of arts and culture spaces.

Majeed took it upon himself to change that: one shack at a time. In 2013, he built two shacks on underutilized plots of land. Faheem programmed his shacks with art that he hoped would speak to the neighborhood.

> You have to think about how do we engage and open space . . . I build platforms for people. . . . I try to think about "who do I want in this shack?" "Who do I want to put at the table to do something engaging in our neighborhoods? In my neighborhood."

Through this project I've worked with one, two, three, four, five different young Black men from the neighborhood. I was very intentional about working with my neighbors. One of the guys, he actually ended up going to jail. He slipped up, but when he got out, we went right back to making shacks.

During my first visit in 2013, the shack at 48th Street and King Drive was covered with plaid plastic material as part of an installation called *Ghana Must Go* by artist Abbey Odunlami. The large squares of material still bore the molded handles from their former life as tote bags. Inside the shack, a small red boombox blasted what sounded like multiple African electro songs layered on top of one another. The seven-foot-tall shack was six feet long, its floor hidden by tote bags, full of what looked like paper or wood.

A then-local artist named Victor Le was taking it all in. I asked him for his impressions.

Well initially, I was just drawn to the architecture of the space. And it makes direct connection because I spent eight months in Accra, Ghana. And so, I'm familiar with this bag. So, it brought back the sentimental feelings. It's a prevalent bag, almost like the brown paper bag of West Africa. You use it for storage. Historically, there was some sort of turmoil between Ghana and Nigeria. And Ghanaians were asked to leave the Nigeria territory [with] these very bags; so, a lot of personal material and objects [were in] these bags. It's very interesting . . . very interesting.[7]

Faheem has a long-vested interest in arts spaces. From 2005 until 2011, he served as executive director of the South Side Community Art Center, the oldest Black arts center of its kind in the country.

As more unconventional spaces spring forth, however, a battle for older Black spaces has increased in its intensity.

Just as it was in the 1960s, there is restlessness among the younger generation of Black Chicago to see the reigns of institutions passed down (if only to assure their survival). But, the civil rights generation, now well into their seventies, are in some cases unwilling to step back from institutions. The result is a generational rift at fever pitch.

And in the particularly public case of the DuSable Museum of African American History, an attempt to put forth a plan for its revitalization was met as an attack.

To me, this seemed like truly a disservice to the legacy of the cofounder of the DuSable, Margaret Burroughs, who like John and Eunice Johnson was extremely forward leaning and committed to building sustainable institutions.

Founded in 1961, the museum has been at its current location since 1973. The first museum of its kind, DuSable served as an archetype for African American museums across the country.

In recent years, however, the museum has struggled through some funding issues. A construction project to expand the campus southward has been in limbo for decades.

In the summer of 2015, a white paper from the DuSable Futures Committee surfaced.[8] The committee was organized by Theaster Gates and Jacqueline Stewart, both members of the faculty of the University of Chicago. Gates was also on the board of DuSable at the time.

The proposal suggested a number of structural and curatorial shifts that would "increase the ambition and inspire a major conceptual shift within one of the most significant culturally specific institutions in the nation."[9]

Journalists Dawn Rhodes and Dahleen Glanton wrote that "the museum downplayed the proposal, saying it was simply Gates' suggestion for a 'growth plan.'"[10]

The DuSable Futures white paper quotes Gates: "There has never been this type of convergence of local leadership, national interest, good will and social commitment to the deep needs of DuSable. We need every citizen of the City to believe that great things can happen here and this institution has limped along long enough." The proposal, which was not intended for public distribution, suggested a need for revamped curatorial practice, deeper activation of the "riches of the institution," and "more rigorous preservation practices."[11]

A group calling itself the Concerned Committee for the Support of Independent Black Cultural Institutions formed, with members including author Lerone Bennett Jr. (who penned many important Black history texts published by Johnson Publishing), Northeastern Illinois University professor Conrad Worrill (of the Carruthers Center for Inner City Studies), and historian Timuel Black. Representative of a respected old guard, their average age surpassed seventy-five. This committee issued a statement that

this proposal [the DuSables Futures white paper] . . . will result in a radical reconceptualization of the ideas, cultural focus, historical knowledge, and critical black direction of the DuSable Museum.

The defining ideas of Dr. Margaret Burroughs and other co-founders of the DuSable Museum are being disregarded and set aside for "new thought" and a "major conceptual shift."[12]

Rhodes and Glanton quoted a younger committee member, Yvette Moyo: "The first place we have to look is in the mirror. . . . What have we done to an institution that is sitting there waiting for us? We have a responsibility, and we have fallen short in owning this institution."[13]

The Concerned Committee commenced an online smear campaign that laid bare the generational divisions that had been so deeply held. It also suggested that Gates was a pawn of the University of Chicago (long seen as an enemy of the Black activist community of the South Side due to various university-funded urban renewal projects that resulted in the fracture of adjacent Black communities). The coalition declared in a letter of intent: "We vehemently disagree with this shift in direction from [museum cofounder] Dr. Margaret Burrough's mission and vision for DuSable Museum. . . . This brazen attempt to deliver the DuSable Museum into University of Chicago management must be immediately halted."[14]

Theaster reacted by pulling back, respectfully.

In a *Chicago Sun-Times* interview, Gates noted:

What has become clear to me is there has been so much disenfranchisement by parts of the black community that the only defense that we have is to fight.

The baton is rarely passed. . . . As a result, our institutions often die, or they flounder. What I don't feel is recognized is I am one of the sons of black radical parents that trained me so I can create new futures. I am doing the work.[15]

Ultimately, some new blood was installed at DuSable, and comparatively small changes to its curatorial practice were met with mostly positive reviews.

Out of the ashes of the DuSable Futures overture grew Theaster Gates's Stony Island Arts Bank, a Black curated space that went from a conception as a holder of cultural artifacts (a cultural bank) to a space that would, additionally, present culture with a gallery on the main floor. Gates presented work by internationally renowned artists such as Noah Davis, James Barnor, and Glenn Ligon. Perhaps indicative of his intentions, he hosted a salon in the space with Thelma Golden of the Studio Museum in Harlem, a well-regarded institution that Golden classified as "Super-Black."[16]

One day, in a dimly lit room, Theaster asked me what I thought his impact had been. This was in 2017. He had accomplished so much, but at that moment he was feeling world-weary.

I told him that the act of staying in the community (doing what he did where he did it) was revolutionary. We'd riffed on this idea a few times together. Once at the Johnson Publishing Library at the Arts Bank, we were talking broadly about how class lines create the perception of distance in the Black community and I mentioned the importance of the aspirational aspect of *Ebony*. Beyond Black celebrities, Black judges, scientists, and entrepreneurs were represented. In this case, the perception of proximity to these people fueled hope for all of us. To put it plainly: because they did, we can.

Back in that dimly lit room, I told him that the things he builds mean something important to people. Not just in terms of access to cultural materials and programming, but in terms of sheer possibility, built out of things that were once called dead. He rebuilds things and places that were considered by most to be down for the count. There must be some allegory in that.

So, it was particularly satisfying to text him a link to an article I read about six months later, "What the Artist Behind Chance the Rapper's Album Art Is Doing for Chicago."[17] The article seemed to me to be a testament to Gates's impact to an artist coming up in the next generation.

Brandon Breaux created the album cover artwork for Chance's mixtapes *10 Day*, *Acid Rap*, *Coloring Book*. He is also an artist whose work and identity are deeply rooted in his South Side Grand Crossing neighborhood.

In the article, Breaux notes how, as a teen, his proximity to the work of other artists made him feel like things were possible for him, too.

The work in Greater Grand Crossing hits home because it's literally where I'm from. I've been an artist since I was born, but I feel like, with cultural identity, sometimes things are assigned to you. A lot of growing and developing was convincing people what else I had to offer besides what they expected from me. It began to change as I matured. When I encountered Gates' work and similar work where people are doing things within com-

138

munities to make a statement and to bring something else to the areas that you are from, it was relieving because it makes you look at the space differently and makes you think about those things differently.[18]

We are in some sort of feedback loop, where the sociopolitical progress folks hoped to see come out of the Black Power era has yet to fully manifest itself. So, what can be drawn from the ideas that were documented in items created to be disposable? Can these imbedded notions fuel progress? Without the filter of academia or the hindsight of a biographer, the immediacy of a *Jet* or a pamphlet for a concert speaks uniquely to their moment of birth. There is value in tracing ideologies from their conception to the apex of their popularity, and then through their evolutions.

A 1970 record released on Stax Records' "Respect" imprint by John KaSandra was called "(What's Under) The Natural Do." An early rap, drenched in organ and bluesy guitar, KaSandra relates, "See, I was black before it was popular / and I wear my natural, too."[19]

Before "Black is Beautiful" was cliché, it was edgy (and controversial to some in the Black community who had long counted "Black" as a slur). In that moment, a statement encapsulated a thirst for positive identity that rejected imported standards of beauty. By the late 1960s, the conk— or straightened look on Black men—was considered a sign of backward thinking. In the same sense, natural hair (which initially incited scorn and shame) became the Afro. The Afro became a political statement, intimately tied to ideas of Black consciousness. And then it wasn't. It became fashionable.

Today, the natural is again en vogue (in all of its iterations). In some communities, those who choose to wear their hair chemically straightened are criticized in much the same way as those pompadoured Black folks of days gone by.

And so the feedback loop coils on.

This feedback loop, this unfinished societal business, is nowhere as evident as in Chicago. Youth violence, police-involved violence, poverty, racial discrimination, open housing, substandard schools: all were issues of paramount importance during the civil rights movement. On the South and West Sides of Chicago, we've gained little ground on these issues in the decades that have followed the initial movement. And, like in the example of resurgence in the popularity of natural hair in the Black community, there are myriad parallels between the post–civil rights era and today.

The historic effort to embrace Blackness is metaphoric for a burgeoning bid to reclaim forsaken communities that is felt here. Media outfits reflect a funhouse mirror that presents Chicago as a lawless spectacle pockmarked by blight and violence.

But where does that toxic story begin? And where does it end?

> What happened to the spirit? Of those captured Africans in that middle passage? On that boat? On that plantation? . . . Everything is passed down parent to child, parent to child, parent to child . . . so just as I have been effected, White America has been effected. —Dr. Frances Cress Love[20]

There is this ghastly legacy, one that can't be excised from the blossoms that have flowered from it.

There is this oppression, not so different from the so-called slum conditions of the middle of the twentieth century. If anything, time and the guise of desegregation have exacerbated the conditions. Buildings that were in disrepair in the 1970s are—if they are even still standing—positively skeletal. Blocks once teeming with life are scarred with vacant lots.

And yet coursing down blocks, pulsing out of speakers in the trunks of candy-colored big-bodied sedans, dreams sizzle and pop. Folks see the occasional dream come true, the Stony Island Arts Bank, or the New Regal Theater, or Chance the Rapper, and they co-opt those dreams to pumice their own world-weary hopes.

We know what can be. We see the Ebony/Jet building, a taupe marble behemoth on Michigan Avenue. And that dream is ours. Those dreams are ours. They will not die. Not as long as we're living.

What we see in most media does not fully reflect the capacity of our collective soul, nor does it reflect the marrow of Black Chicago.

To be true to that marrow, we must allow younger people the latitude to push what has been built forward into the next phase, rather than let this energy languish (or worse, still) dissipate.

Fortunately, according to the wisdom of Earth, Wind & Fire and their classic "I'll Write a Song For You," "Sounds, they never dissipate / They only recreate / In another space and time."[21] The same can be said for energy.

For a time during the late 1960s, the Vice Lords shifted from being a powerful street gang into an equally powerful street organization called the Conservative Vice Lords, filling storefronts on the West Side with community-focused enterprises.

Bona fide gangsters recognizing their might and opening an art center and a Tastee-Freez franchise. They even opened a management training institute, proving that energy is absolute, and can be channeled in myriad directions.

CVL were ten thousand strong in 1968, and gang-related violence had dropped dramatically. But, by the spring of 1969, the city administration declared a war on gangs.

DeWitt Beall's 1970 film on the CVL, *Lord Thing*, features CVL acting president Kenneth "Goat" Parks, who in 1969 declared, "[Mayor Richard J. Daley is] afraid of the whole projection that [the gangs] can become politically involved. Or form the kind of economic base that someone else may have to deal with. He's afraid of us going and becoming constructive."[22]

The CVL movement was fatally derailed when Vice Lord Spokesman Bobby Gore was convicted of murder in a 1969 crackdown that targeted Gore and Leonard Sengali, as well as Alfonso Alfred, then-president of the CVL. In December of that year, Fred Hampton, the twenty-one-year-old charismatic chairman of the Illinois chapter of the Black Panthers, was killed in his bed by police in an overnight raid. Not long after Gore was imprisoned, the Vice Lords reverted to being a violent street gang.

Right now, there are young Black men, not unlike those Vice Lords, that are expending violent, angry energy across Chicago. That energy counters so much of the good that is happening here. Despite media portrayals, negative energy is not the most prominent force in Black Chicago, but it underscores so much around us. It lurks.

However, it doesn't have to be that way.

The latent power of Afro-optimism lies in its ability to suspend disbelief, to allow space for faith in an alternate reality. That faith is still here. Creativity, hustle, and a belief in the impossible are still here.

And so are we.

One March morning, a day on the verge of spring, I was talking with a mid-twenty-something Julian Reid of the Juju Exchange who had at one time served as a prison chaplain. He was quick to tell a story that so clearly demonstrates how the optimistic energy he feels tied to also sustains him.

JULIAN REID: So I was working in the prison . . . hard day, particularly hard day. I don't remember the specifics, but I just came home and was exhausted of how I had given myself and of myself in this chaplaincy program with these kids [juvenile defenders]. And the one thing I wanted to listen to was not a gospel song, it wasn't something really peaceful or anything like that.

I wanted to listen to the song that [Juju Exchange] had written, "Morning Of." It's the first song on our record *Exchange*. And I specifically wanted to listen, not even to my solo, but I wanted to listen to [Nico Segal's] horns. He has these horns that come at about 2:20, 2:21. And man, when they come on, they are just so arresting, which is ironic—an ironic word to use here. But they just, they hold my attention and lift me in a way that I can't explain, just got to go listen to the music, but in a way that I so needed in that moment. I knew I needed that in that moment seeing what I had just seen with those kids.

What I hope our music can do is thread this needle between these currents that seek to either keep Black folk criminalized or seek to only placate us with a certain kind of Black boy joy. How can you hold together the world as it is?

There's this theologian I like, Karl Barth, who wrote this music, wrote this book on Mozart—he was obsessed with Mozart. And he talks about how Mozart plays the world as it is. He's not overly optimistic, not pessimistic. He plays the world with its discord and you hear, you hear the light and the dark fuse together. And I think that, when you can hear that kind of fusion in a way that points to hope, hope that something can be different, not necessarily a naive optimism that somebody won't get shot today, but that you hope that something could fundamentally change about this country, I think music and I would even say particularly music without words can really help drive people to that place of desiring, of longing.

And there was something in that moment, having coming out of the prisons, seeing all that I was seeing week after week with these kids, something just sitting in my car and my parking lot at home and listening to Nico's horns on this song called "Morning Of," what's the morning of what, morning or freedom, morning of new beginnings, morning of a changeover, morning of an overhaul, whatever it is, the morning of, I felt that, and I really, really, really want our audiences to feel that. Just like audiences felt that back in the '60s and '70s, . . . I want cats to feel that now. And there's something hard that you have to do in order [to] get that from wordless music because it doesn't have the kind of . . . it doesn't have the immediate recognition value that you get from words. But, if you can sit and let yourself be engulfed in what these sounds can create of how they can play the world as it is and the world as it can be, I think that there's something unique there that can really change a lot.

AYANA CONTRERAS: [*Interjecting*] Yeah. And I think because we're a literate society, generally literate, word-based, I think what happens is we get caught up in the words, and we don't even realize the magic that's happening with the music.

As you were telling that story, I was also thinking about the album *Curtis* from 1970. And there's lots of songs that [illustrate this]. But I'm thinking particularly of "We the People Who Are Darker than Blue," and the way that the score underneath that song really has this forward momentum that pulls you into all these different places and spaces with just the instrumental track.

. . . Curtis [Mayfield] is saying a whole lot in that song. But then if you even take those lyrics out and you just focus on what's happening with the horns, what's happening with [Master Henry Gibson's] Congas, what's happening with Lucky Scott [playing bass], . . . you know what I'm saying?

JR: [*Nodding*] That's beautiful. Well, I appreciate the fact that you're trying to draw these strong ties between then and now. And I think that that kind of attention to history is something that the people need. And by "people," I mean broadly young musicians who are coming up who are only being taught in music school how to execute scales, not being taught at all about the history of the music, about how their teachers got in front of them, etc., as well as older folk, the seasoned folk who may have a real handle on the '60s and '70s but might be confused or dismayed or whatever else about the current status.

And of course, I mean, these are caricatures, people are complex and everybody's in the middle of something. But I think that being able to draw a bridge with your research between then and now can help all parties involved. And so I'm really looking forward to being able to read it, sit with it and figure out how my own lineage and how I've understood my . . . tributaries, how that fits into this really broad river of black music in Chicago. But then of course, because if it's black folk in Chicago, it's probably black folk in the South, and of course you're going back to the continent. So there's just all kinds of points of connection between what we're doing now and then this huge jump-off point of the '60s and '70s into our past.[23]

﹆ ﹅ ﹇

I once saw a T-shirt that read "I am my ancestors' wildest dreams." There is an audacity in the aspirational. In the aspirational, there is also the prospect of living vicariously through the dizzying highs of others. There is power in the idea that, one day, the world might be ours for the taking, too. And, there is indisputable power in the notion that our individual stories of overcoming, however modest, are part of an overarching epic exemplified by Black Chicago.

In the summer of 2007, I headed off to play the numbers, or the lottery, for my Grandmother Phyllis Flowers. Pausing from shucking sweet corn at the kitchen table, she wrote down what she wanted—"a dollar straight, one quick pick, little lotto"—on a scrap of paper. I had no idea what those words meant.

At the time, I felt as though three dollars spent playing numbers could be spent on something else where you've got half a chance of actually making it happen.

"A dollar straight, one quick pick, little lotto," I mumbled on my way to her Toyota, keys jingling in hand. "I feel like I'm speaking another language."

Luck. It's a notion that's only as palpable as the vague grease and meaty smell that wafts from the Polish sausage spot that stood on a corner near her house. The seagulls ate French fries from a ragged paper bag in the parking lot, an expanse of cracked asphalted sea, and another notion haunted me. Why does the lottery stir up this worry in me? Is the cult of luck the villain?

"And then, two Longboys." I ordered through bulletproof glass. Back then, I had a taste for the chewy caramel and coconut confections, wrapped in yellow waxed paper.

The South Asian cashier replied, "Yeah, forty cents. Gimme three dollars for lottery. And forty cents for those."

"Okay."

As I slipped the cash through a tiny opening between us, I noticed our skin is the same tone of brown. Beeps pulsed musically as he rang up the purchase. He slid a few coins worth of change toward me. They clanged like a tambourine against the metal countertop.

In Black American churches around the country, around the time that crack cocaine and Reaganomics were unleashed on the inner city like tandem rabid dogs, the "prosperity message" broke a gaggle of chains. Where the martyrdom of poverty once reigned and the meek inherited the earth, once-carnal desires for wealth were legitimized from the pulpit. Being rich was holy. Being poor was a result of some sort of spiritual disconnect. And luck was a lie. Blessings were counted in dollars and cents.

The message took hold, despite contrary biblical verses like Luke 12:15, where Jesus warns us to "beware of covetousness, for one's life does not consist in the abundance of the things he possesses."

Still, stronger grew the desire to accumulate wealth, as the taboo of flash faded. Sanctified and sullied both, pockets of peppermints and motel matchbooks, all gathered in line come Monday, their collection of numbers holding promises. To the sanctified, it held the promise of heaven on earth; and to the sullied, it held a ticket to a place called Away.

At Nat King Cole Park, at 83rd Street and South Calumet Avenue on Chicago's South Side, I spoke with a fifty-something Black man seated on a park bench.

AYANA CONTRERAS: My grandmother sent me off to the gas station to play the numbers. And I'm thinking to myself . . . like today, she feels lucky. Now if she doesn't win, will she feel less lucky? Does that make sense? I never understood the reason for the lottery. Do you ever go?"

MAN: Of course. [*Continues, half-jokingly.*] "You can't win if you don't play"— referencing the longtime catchphrase of the Illinois State Lottery.

AC: So, can you explain the psychology behind that? [The sound of beautiful brown children playing rings in the background.]

MAN: I don't believe in luck myself. What I thought at one time was luck, I found out later was divine intervention. . . . Just like if you get into a car accident and walk away without a scratch and say "Oh, I was lucky." God just wasn't ready for you then. [*Chuckles.*]

At first blush, the lottery seemed villainous to me. How many dollars are seemingly wasted from people who truly need them? People who measure life in single dollars rather than in hundreds of dollars. To me they were buying nothing, relishing in wafting strains of luck.

But in the United States in particular, the lottery (sometimes referred to by the somewhat inaccurate antiquated term "the numbers") has represented a chance at mobility for people of color that was otherwise nearly impossible. In addition to presenting the hope of a jackpot, numbers kingpins became ad hoc lenders in communities where people of color were not afforded loans from traditional banks.

Bolita is Spanish for "little ball," and it's also a lottery that involves one hundred numbered ivory balls that are placed in a sack (historically velvet), then the balls are drawn out.[24] Bets are placed on what numbers will surface.

The game was particularly popular in South Florida (particularly Ybor City and Tampa, and later Miami) from the later nineteenth century until the mid-twentieth century. Playing bolita was especially widespread among Latinos, Blacks, and Italians. The bolita racket was generally run by the local mafia.

Cheating was commonplace. Sometimes, specific balls were chilled first, allowing the person drawing them to feel for certain balls. Other times, specific balls were filled with lead, also making them easier to identify. Another means to rig the game was by adding extra balls with a particular number.

In some Latino communities, a method of understanding the numbers drawn is known as *la Charada*. In la charada, each number represents something. For instance, number 83 might represent *tragedia* (tragedy), or 87 might represent *platano* (a cooking banana).

Bolita took root in Cuba, as well, and though it's been illegal since the Revolution, it remains popular.

In early twentieth-century New York City, running numbers was a means for sky-high socioeconomic advancement. Stephanie St. Clair of Martinique was a one-time maid who overcame debilitating abuse from a series of men to become a mob boss in 1920s Harlem.[25]

Chicago's Prohibition-era mafia enterprises are infamous, but other means of monetizing luck rose from the South Side of Chicago in the early twentieth century.

Founded by a Jewish chemist named Morton Neumann, Valmor Products Company sold perfumes, incense, creams, and other products. Many of the products carried names tied to southern American Hoodoo, such as Follow Me Boy perfume (named after a particular Hoodoo spell). But there were also items more explicitly tied to southern Hoodoo, or root work. In 1944, for only one dollar, you could purchase an "Alleged Root Doctor's Hand" detailed in a mail-order catalog:

> a red flannel bag that contained Sampson Snake Root, "Devil's Shoe String," magnetic lodestone, High John the Conqueror Root, one Witches' Dream Book, and Yellow Brimstone.[26]

According to the description,

> This was first wrapped in Black Cloth folded always towards the maker, and then encased in a red flannel bag. The conjure man said it should be wet with whiskey or camphor at regular intervals and carried with you. It was stated that such a bag brings things to you and twine-like roots of Devil's Shoe Strings ties them close and folding of the cover towards you insures you good luck in gambling.[27]

The products gained nationwide customers via mail-order catalogs, and both the catalogs and the product labels bore eye-catching, romantic illustrations: more than a few pictured raven-haired, racially ambiguous women, bent back in an embrace with equally lovestruck, racially ambiguous men.[28]

Cosmetics are often thought of as recession-proof, even pandemic-proof, as 2020 showed us. No matter how hard times are, people will make a way to fold a bit of magic or glamour into their lives. During rough times, such magic can be even more valued because it represents momentary respite, or a taste of another life. Naturally, Valmor products, which were essentially traditional Hoodoo recipes reimagined as toiletries, did well for many years.

Back at Nat King Cole Park, in 2007, on the South Side of Chicago, beneath a shade tree, I approached a woman.

AYANA CONTRERAS: Do you believe in luck? Do you think it's real?
WOMAN: I believe in it using a different term. Like things are supposed to happen as they do, and it may seem like luck. Or it might seem like

a coincidence, but it's kind of on track of happening. It's kind of . . . You attract certain things to you, that it happens that way. So, luck, or good fortune, or blessings, or synchronicity, you know, any of those things, it's kind of synonymous with luck, I think. With luck being kind of more chance-y. But, if it's meant for you it happens . . . If it's not meant for you to happen, it won't happen for you.

AC: [*Tentatively*] So, kind of like destiny?

WOMAN: [*Nodding*] Kind of like that. And you can think of something happening or wanting something to happen you kind of attract it to you. Say, like, you say "Mmm. I sure would like a piece of cake." And your mother says, "Oh I just made some cake. Why don't you come by and pick up some?" You know, some things you attract, I believe. Sometimes we can kind of ask things to happen for us, and it happens, in that way.

AC: [*Confiding*] The reason why I'm doing this [asking people about the idea of luck], is my grandmother sent me off to go pick her numbers. I have a thing against the numbers. I feel like us spending our money on the numbers . . .

WOMAN: I'm with it. I agree. I understand. [*Nodding.*] My dad was on his dying bed, and he asked me to go play some numbers for him.

So that was the moment. I pictured her father lying in bed between percale sheets, the smell of death (sort of like mildew in a linen closet) looming over him. And on his dying bed, he asked her to go buy his lottery ticket. But in that moment, it hit me. Maybe I was wrong. Maybe it's not about luck at all. Maybe it's about reaching out toward the future. Maybe Black folks who play the numbers, like her father, are just sacrificing at the altar of dreams. And he just wanted to dream one more time.

So, there is no end. What has been passed down in Black Chicago is Afro-optimism. The power to believe the definition of Blackness that was bred here is not a myth. To believe that we can burst through obstacles and make ways out of no way. This is not a bootstrap myth. This is a story of averages. It could happen to us, too. . . . . Because it happened here. It's in the water. It's in us all. There's proof of sheer possibility all around us. Happenings akin to sho nuff miracles willed into existence. At least that's what Grandma says. And that is as real as a royal-blue jar of Ultra Sheen conditioning hair dress.

NOTES

Preface

The preface epigraph is from Theaster Gates, "Kerry James Marshall," *New York Times Style Magazine*, video, October 17, 2016, https://www.nytimes.com.

1. Venson Cunningham, "The Argument of Afropessimism," *New Yorker*, July 20, 2020.

2. Fred Moten, "Black Optimism/Black Operation," 2007, unpublished paper on file with the author. Later quotations by Moten in this preface are also from this source.

3. Ebere Onwudiwe, "Introduction: A Context for Post-Colonial African Discourse," in *Afro-Optimism: Perspectives on Africa's Advances*, ed. Ebere Onwudiwe and Minabere Ibelema (Westport, CT: Praeger, 2003), 4.

4. Rev. William H. Borders, "I Am Somebody," in *Rhetoric of Racial Revolt*, edited by Roy L. Hill, 337 (Denver: Golden Bell, 1964).

5. Naomi Beckwith, interview with the author, Chicago, April 2018.

6. Curtis Mayfield, "Move On Up," on *Curtis* LP, Curtom Records, 1970.

7. "Closing Ranks on Poverty: Cooperatives Give New Hope to Poor People of South," *Ebony*, August 1971, 96.

i. On Stony Island Avenue

1. Mary Owen, "Leon Finney Sr.: 1916-2008," *Chicago Tribune*, April 6, 2008.

2. "Chicago's New Regal Theater Debuts with Weeklong Gala," *Jet*, September 7, 1987, 56-58.

3. Dianna Budds, "The Stony Island Arts Bank Brings 'Redemptive Architecture' to Chicago's South Side," *Fast Company*, October 6, 2015, https://www.fastcompany.com, accessed February 5, 2021.

4. Doris Duke Charitable Foundation, Self Grantee Reports, Columbia College, 1., https://www.ddcf.org/globalassets/Arts/Grantee-Self-Reports/Columbia-College.pdf, accessed March 28, 2021.

5. Description of *The Destruction of Civilization* by Chancellor Williams, Third World Press, https://thirdworldpressfoundation.org/product/destruction-of-black-civilization, accessed February 5, 2021.

6. Rozzell Sykes, in *Black Omnibus*, episode 6, hosted by James Earl Jones, directed by Donald I. Davis, aired 1973 on PBS.

7. Robin D. G. Kelley, *Freedom Dreams: The Black Radical Imagination* (Boston: Beacon, 2002), 2.

8. Heb. 11:1 (AV).

9. Mumbo Sauce advertisement, *Life*, circa 1970, https://live-selectbrands.pantheonsite.io/about-mumbo-sauce/history/, accessed January 24, 2010.

ii. Sort of a Dream

1. "How King Wages War on Slums in Chicago," *Jet*, February 10, 1966, 14–20. Later quotations from *Jet* in this chapter are from this article.

2. "Photo-Editorial: It's Love, Love, Love," *Ebony*, July 1967, 100–101.

3. Dr. Martin Luther King Jr. interviewed by Wesley South on *Wesley South's Hotline*, WVON (Chicago), aired July 1966.

4. Otis Spann, "A Tribute to Martin Luther King," performed with Muddy Waters, Cry Records (Apostle Music Corp.), produced by Norman Dayron, 3:40 min., 1968.

5. Norine L. Smith, "Channel 5's Warner Saunders from Activist to Anchor," *Chicago Reporter*, March 1992, 34.

6. Ibid.

7. Louie Robinson, "TV Discovers the Black Man," *Ebony*, February 1969, 27-35.

8. "Black TV: Its Problems and Promises," *Ebony*, September 1969, 88-94. Later quotations from *Ebony* in this chapter are from this article.

9. "Jim Tilmon's Our People," *Chicago Stories*, https://interactive.wttw.com/, accessed February 8, 2021.

10. Interview by Richard Steele, "West Side Legends: George Daniels, Gus Rickette, and Charmaine Alfred," episode 141, *The Barber Shop Show*, Vocalo 91.1FM, aired October 9, 2013. Later quotations by Daniels, Charmaine Alfred, and Gus Rickette in this chapter are from this interview.

11. Rufus Williams interviewed by Richard Steele, "Making the West Side," episode 280, *The Barber Shop Show*, Vocalo 91.1FM, aired September 15, 2016.

12. Robert Townsend interviewed by the author on *Reclaimed Soul*, Los Angeles, Vocalo 91.1FM, aired August 20, 2018. Later quotations by Townsend in this chapter are from this interview.

13. On Jae Jarrell's influence, see David Lusenhop, *Jae Jarrell and the Fashioning of Black Culture* (Cleveland: Museum of Contemporary Art Cleveland, 2015), 70.

14. *The Black Fairy*, LP, released by LaMont Zeno Theatre Foundation on BBF Records (private label), 1975. Later quotations from *The Black Fairy* in this chapter are from the LP.

15. "Chico Freeman in Chicago Jazz Magazine: In His Own Words," Chico Freeman, https://chicofreeman.com/chico-freeman-in-chicago-jazz-magazine-in-his-own-words/.

iii. Found

1. Curtis Mayfield quoted in "From the Vantage Point of a New Album, *America Today*, Curtis Mayfield Looks Back at 17 Years of Hits," *Circular* 7, no. 18 (May 12, 1975): 1-6; later Mayfield quotations in this chapter are from this source. The Impressions, "It's All Right," ABC-Paramount, 1964, 45 rpm.

2. avery r. young, personal interview by the author, Chicago, May 2018.

3. Curtis Mayfield, "People Get Ready," on *Rapping*, promotional recording, Curtom, 1972, LP.

4. "We're a Winner," words and music by Curtis Mayfield, performed by the Impressions, ABC-Paramount, 1967, 45 rpm.

5. Curtis Mayfield quoted in "From the Vantage Point."

6. "This Is My Country," words and music by Curtis Mayfield, performed by the Impressions, Curtom Records, 1968, 45 rpm.

7. Todd Mayfield, unedited interview audiotaped by the author, Chicago, October 2016, for *Reclaimed Soul*, Chicago, Vocalo 91.1FM.

8. Naomi Beckwith, personal interview by the author, Chicago, April 2018.

9. Curtis Mayfield quoted in "From the Vantage Point."

10. "We Got to Have Peace," words and music by Curtis Mayfield, Curtom Records, 1971, 45 rpm.

11. Lee Bey, "A Saint in Need of a Savior: Old St. Laurence Parish," *WBEZ Blogs*, June 14, 2010, https://www.wbez.org, accessed June 4, 2014.

12. "Preservation Chicago Unveils the 2011 Chicago 7 Most Threatened: St. Laurence Church," Preservation Chicago, n.d., https://preservationchicago.org, accessed February 13, 2021.

13. Landmarks Illinois, http://landmarks.org/ten_most, accessed May 2010.

14. "St. Laurence Demolition Segment with Ayana Contreras," *Afternoon Shift*, WBEZ, aired June 17, 2014.

15. Bhaskhar Mazumder, "Black-White Differences in Intergenerational Economic Mobility in the United States Economic Perspectives," *Economic Perspectives* 38, no. 1 (2014), https://papers.ssrn.com/sol3/papers.cfm?abstract_id=2434178, accessed March 29, 2021.

16. Mary Pattillo, *Black Picket Fences: Privilege and Peril among the Black Middle Class* (Chicago: University of Chicago Press, 1999), 1.

17. Dennis Rodkin, "The Rebuilders of Chicago's Southland," *Crain's Chicago Business*, April 24, 2017, https://www.chicagobusiness.com/static/section/rebuilders.html, accessed May 1, 2017.

iv. *Stax Fax*

1. Deanie Parker, ed., *Stax Fax*, December 1969.

2. Kate Sierzputowski, "A Procession of Black Love Responds to Controversial Michael Brown Exhibition in Chicago," Hyperallergic, September 7, 2015, https://hyperallergic .com, accessed February 13, 2021.

3. Rev. William H. Borders, "I Am Somebody," in *Rhetoric of Racial Revolt*, edited by Roy L. Hill, 337 (Denver: Golden Bell, 1964).

4. "I'm Somebody," composed by Wayne Readus and C. Johnson, performed by Original Breed, Karol Records, 1968, 45 rpm.

5. Wayne Readus, interview by Bob Abrahamian, *Sitting in the Park*, WHPK (Chicago), aired January 8, 2006.

6. "I Am Somebody," performed by the Brothers and Sisters, Toddlin Town Records, 1969, 45 rpm.

7. "Black Christmas 1968," *Stax Fax*, December 1969, 25.

8. Sidney Barnes, telephone interview by the author on *Reclaimed Soul*, Vocalo 91.1FM, aired November, 2007.

9. Ibid.

10. "This Christmas," composed by Donny Hathaway, lyrics by Nadine McKinnor and Donny Hathaway (credited as "Donny Pitts"), performed by Donny Hathaway (vocals), Ric Powell (congas and bass drums), Willie Henderson (saxophone), Phil Upchurch (electric guitar), Louis Satterfield (trombone), and Morris Jennings (drums), Atco Records, 1970, 45 rpm.

11. "(I'm Going Back To) Live in the City," performed by Carla Thomas, Stax Records, 1970, 45 rpm.

12. Dave Hoekstra, "Remembering 'This': Hathaway's Classic Carol," *Chicago Sun-Times*, December 13, 2009.

13. Christopher Borrelli, "'This Christmas': How a Chicago Postal Worker and Donny Hathaway Created a Holiday Classic," *Chicago Tribune*, December 20, 2017, https:// www.chicagotribune.com, accessed May 14, 2018.

14. Ric Powell quoted in Hoekstra, "Remembering 'This.'"

15. "Black Christmas," written by Pervis Staples, performed by the Emotions, Volt Records, 1970, 45 rpm.

16. Martin Luther King Jr. quoted in Jonathan Rieder, *The Word of the Lord Is upon Me: The Righteous Performance of Martin Luther King, Jr.* (Cambridge, MA: Belknap Press of Harvard University Press, 2008), 52-53.

17. "Black Christmas," Volt, 1970.

18. "Breadbasket Launches 2nd Black Christmas," *Woodlawn Observer*, 6, no. 33 (December 4, 1969): 1.

19. Ibid., 1.

20. "Black Christmas," Volt, 1970.

21. "Black Christmas 1968," 25.

22. "Black Easter," *Stax Fax*, December 1969, 26-29.

23. See Claire Voon, "An Art Exhibition Featuring Michael Brown's Body Has Many People Angry," *Hyperallergic*, July 14, 2015.

24. Sierzputowski, "Procession of Black Love."

25. Christopher Borrelli, "The Complicated Exodus of Art World Star Cauleen Smith," *Chicago Tribune*, August 18, 2017.

26. Cauleen Smith, "Human_3.0 Reading List," https://readinglisthumanthree pointo.wordpress.com/2015/06/15/june-16-2015/, accessed February 14, 2021.

V. All This Talk about Freedom

1. Patricia Lathion, "Black Stone Rangers," in *Our Voice: Poetry by Black Children* ([Chicago:] Free Black Press, [1968?]), n.p.

2. Oscar Brown Jr., interviewed by Porter James and Rick Wojcik. *Roctober* 15 (1996), http://roctober.com/roctober/greatness/obj (dead), accessed July 1, 2011.

3. James Alan McPherson, "Chicago's Blackstone Rangers (Part 1)," *Atlantic*, May 1969, https://www.theatlantic.com, accessed December 28, 2011.

4. "Radio-TV," *Jet*, January 25, 1968, 66.

5. "Opportunity Please Knock: Youth Gang Produces Lively Show with Guidance of Oscar Brown, Jr.," *Ebony*, August 1967, 104.

6. Maggie Brown interviewed by the author on *Reclaimed Soul*, Chicago, Vocalo 91.1FM, aired March 9, 2017.

7. "All This Talk about Freedom," written by G. Lewis, performed by the Opportunity Please Knock Chorus, arranged by Cleveland Eaton, produced by Harvey J. Coombs, Ramsel Records 68-100, 1968, 45 rpm, 3:08 min.

8. Carol Marin, dir., *Angel of Fear*, documentary, WMAQ-TV, broadcast June 27, 1988.

9. DeWitt Beall, dir., *Lord Thing*, documentary, 16 mm film, 1970. Later quotations from *Lord Thing* in this chapter are from this film.

10. J. R. Jones, "A Chicago Street Gang Tries to Go Straight in *Lord Thing*," *Chicago Reader*, July 30, 2014, https://www.chicagoreader.com, accessed December 14, 2018.

11. "The Week's Best Photos," *Jet*, October 30, 1969, 43.

12. Jerry Butler, "Black Music Is Getting Intellectually Involved," *Billboard*, August 22, 1970, 18.

13. Gene Chandler interviewed by the author on *Reclaimed Soul*, Chicago, Vocalo 91.1FM, aired 2008.

14. "Chicago—To Build a Creative Soul Center," *Billboard*, August 22, 1970, 20-22.

15. Gene Ford, "Black," in *Our Voice*, n.p.

1. Miles Marshall Lewis, *There's a Riot Goin' On* (New York: Bloomsbury Academic, 2006), 73.

2. Kate Brown, "'Black People Figured Out How to Make Culture in Freefall': Arthur Jafa on the Creative Power of Melancholy," *Artnet*, February 2018, https://news.artnet.com/, accessed February 17, 2021.

3. For more on the tamale in Chicago, see Mike Sula, "The Great Tamale Migration," *Chicago Reader*, September 16, 2013, https://www.chicagoreader.com, accessed February 17, 2021.

4. Allison Collins interviewed by the author on *Reclaimed Soul*, Vocalo 91.1FM, aired April 2008. Later quotations by Collins in this chapter are from this interview.

5. James Lemons interviewed by Amy Evans, Chicago Eats/TABASCO Guardians of the Tradition, Chicago, March 26, 2008, https://www.southernfoodways.org/interview/lems-bar-b-q, accessed April 29, 2015.

6. Lloyd King interviewed by the author on *Reclaimed Soul*, Vocalo 91.1FM, aired April 2008.

7. Garland Green interview by the author on *Reclaimed Soul*, Vocalo 91.1FM, aired November 2009.

8. Robert Pruter, *Chicago Soul* (Urbana: University of Illinois Press, 1991), 5.

9. Earl Paige, "Chicago's Chess—Moving Out to New York, Los Angeles," *Billboard*, August 22, 1970, 25-26.

10. Marshall Chess interviewed by the author on *Reclaimed Soul*, Chicago, Vocalo 91.1FM, aired October 2007. Later quotations by Chess in this chapter are from this interview.

11. Sidney Barnes, telephone interview by the author on *Reclaimed Soul*, Vocalo 91.1FM, aired November 2007. Later quotations by Barnes in this chapter are from this interview.

12. Maurice White, with Herb Powell, *My Life with Earth, Wind & Fire* (New York: Amistad/HarperCollins, 2016), 54-55, 63-68. Much of the background information on the group comes from White.

13. Sam Sutherland, "Maurice White: From Sessionman to Producer," *Record World*, January 7, 1978, 36-42.

14. Pharaohs, *The Awakening*, Scarab Records, 1971, LP.

15. Pharaohs, "Freedom Road," words and music by Charles Handy, side B of "Love And Happiness," Scarab Records, 1972, 45 rpm, 2:49 min.

16. Rotary Connection, "I Am the Black Gold of the Sun," words and music by Charles Stepney and Richard Rudolph, on *Hey Love*, Cadet Concept Records, 1971, LP.

17. Earth, Wind & Fire, "Keep Your Head to the Sky," words and music by Maurice White, Columbia Records, 1973, LP.

18. Earth, Wind & Fire, *Spirit*, inner sleeve, Columbia Records, LP, 1976.

19. Natalie Cole interviewed by Richard Steele, WJPC-AM, aired December 1, 1977. Later quotations by Cole and Steele in this chapter are from this interview.

20. Otis Clay, personal interview by the author, Chicago, January 2013. Later quotations by Clay in this chapter are from this interview.

vii. It's a Tom Tom, Part 2

1. "I'll Write a Song for You," words and music by Philip Bailey, Stephen Beckmeier, and Albert McKay, on *All 'n All* LP, Columbia Records, 1977.

2. "Tom Tom Washington Credits Discography," *Discogs*, https://www.discogs.com/artist/277890-Tom-Tom-84, accessed November 2017.

3. Otis Clay, personal interview by the author, Chicago, January 2013. Later quotations by Clay in this chapter are from this interview.

4. Tom Tom Washington and Gene Barge interviewed by the author on *Reclaimed Soul*, Chicago, Vocalo 91.1FM, aired May 2013. Later quotations by Washington and Barge in this chapter are from this interview.

5. Reggie Torian Sr., interviewed by the author on *Reclaimed Soul*, Chicago, Vocalo 91.1FM, aired November 2013.

6. On the history of AACM, see, for example, "About AACM," AACM Chicago, aacmchicago.org/about, accessed April 28, 2018; and George E. Lewis, *A Power Stronger than Itself: The AACM and American Experimental Music* (Chicago: University of Chicago Press, 2008).

7. Junius Paul, personal interview by the author, Chicago, April 2018. Later quotations by Paul in this chapter are from this interview.

8. Ben LaMar Gay, personal interview by the author, Chicago, May 2018. Later quotations by Gay in this chapter are from this interview.

9. Winter Jazzfest, New York City, January 12, 2019; see https://www.winterjazzfest.com.

10. Julian Reid, personal interview by the author, Chicago, April 2018. Later quotations by Reid in this chapter are from this interview.

11. Ayana Contreras, author's prewritten speech for Chicago Overground Showcase, Winterjazz Fest, 2019. Later quotations in this chapter from this talk are from the same source.

12. Chance the Rapper, "Prom Night," on *10 Day* mixtape, private label, 2012.

viii. Visions of Soul

1. Lou Rawls interviewed by Don Cornelius, episode 207, *Soul Train*, hosted by Don Cornelius, Don Cornelius Productions, WCIU-TV, aired January 22, 1977.

2. See also Jake Austen, "Soul Train Local," *Chicago Reader*, October 2, 2008, https://www.chicagoreader.com, accessed October 6, 2008.

3. Berry Gordy, dir., *Mahogany*, Motown Productions/Paramount, 1975.

4. "Entertainment Page," *Carolina Times*, November 8, 1975, 12.

5. Ivan Dixon, dir., *The Spook Who Sat by the Door*, United Artists, 1973.

6. Nina Metz, "New Doc Unearths Story behind Making of 'The Spook Who Sat by the Door,'" *Chicago Tribune*, August 18, 2011, https://www.chicagotribune.com, accessed February 19, 2021.

7. Arthur Marks, dir., *Monkey Hustle*, American International Pictures, 1976.

8. Todd Mayfield, unedited interview audiotaped by the author, Chicago, October 2016, for *Reclaimed Soul*, Chicago, Vocalo 91.1FM.

9. Curtis Mayfield, "Pusherman," on *Rapping*, Curtom, 1972, LP.

10. Todd Mayfield interview.

11. Mayfield, "Pusherman."

ix. Brand-New You

1. Haki R. Madhubuti, writing as Don L. Lee, "The Black Writer and the Black Community," *Black World*, May 1972, 86.

2. Ibid., 87.

3. "Black Family Victims of Cross-Burning After TV Show on Ku Klux Klan," *Jet*, September 9, 1977, 13.

4. Lerone Bennett Jr., "Of Time, Space, and Revolution," *Ebony*, August 1969, 34.

5. *Black Minorities Business and Cultural Expo Program*, October 3, 1969, author's personal collection.

6. Alfred A. Edmond Jr., "Should Black Businesses Be Sold to Whites?," *Black Enterprise*, November 1993, 45-47.

7. Robert E. Johnson, "The Prodigal Returns to His First Love: The Beauty Industry," *Jet*, November 6, 1975, 20-25.

8. Ibid., 20.

9. Ibid., 22.

10. Ibid., 22.

11. "First Ultra Sheen Beauty Boutique Unveils in Chicago," *Jet*, April 14, 1977, 9.

12. "George Johnson Opens First Ultra Sheen Beauty Boutique," *Jet*, June 23, 1977, 15.

13. Leon Dash, "Johnson's New African Market," *Black Enterprise*, March 1981, 19.

14. Leon Dash, "Smugglers in Their Hair," *Black Enterprise*, August 1982, 18.

15. Susan Chandler, "Divorce Triggers Change in Leadership at JPC," *Black Enterprise*, December 1989, 17.

16. Mark R. Wilson, "Cosmetics and Hair Care Products," *Encyclopedia of Chicago*, http://www.encyclopedia.chicagohistory.org, accessed February 22, 2021.

17. C. J. Rewick, "Soft Sheen Sale Near," *Crain's Chicago Business*, April 25, 1998.

18. "New You in '82," words and music by Willis, Colbert, and Young, vocals by Sheila Hutchinson, Soft Sheen Records 201023, promotional disk, 1982, 45 rpm.

19. "Soft Sheen Launches Series on WJPC Radio in Chicago," *Jet*, March 1, 1982, 64.

20. Ibid.

21. Details on Fulton are from "Dr. Alvenia Fulton, 92, Famed Nutritionist, Dies in Chicago," *Jet*, March 22, 1999, 18, and Diane Struzzi, "Natural Healer Alvenia Fulton," *Chicago Tribune*, March 20, 1999, https://www.chicagotribune.com, accessed April 23, 2018.

22. "The Beginning of the Void," performed by Danny Hunt, words and music by G. Davis, arranged by G. Davis, produced by Bob Pittman, La Cade Records 1001-B, 1973.

23. *Roux Laboratories, Inc. v. La Cade Products Co.*, 558 F.2d 33 (1977).

24. Yvette Caslin, "Jory Luster Celebrates Family Hair Care Brand's 60th Anniversary with Pride," *Rolling Out*, April 29, 2017, https://rollingout.com, accessed April 9, 2018.

25. Robert Pruter, *Chicago Soul* (Urbana: University of Illinois Press, 1991), 237-42.

26. David T. Beito and Linda Royster, *Black Maverick: T. R. M. Howard's Fight for Civil Rights and Economic Power* (Urbana: University of Illinois Press, 2009).

27. Ronald Kisner and Warren Brown, "Will the SCLC Split Kill Dr. King's Dream?," *Jet*, January 13, 1972, 12-15. "Robinson Quits Chicago SCLC Breadbasket Post," *Jet*, August 17, 1973, 45.

28. "Races: Black Expo in Chicago," *Time*, October, 11, 1971, http://www.time.com, accessed April 25, 2009.

29. Stan Lathan, dir., *Save the Children*, documentary, Paramount Pictures, 1973, 123 min.

30. "Races: Black Expo in Chicago."

31. Ray Quintanilla, "Black Expo: Taking Care of Business?," *Chicago Reporter*, September 1993, http://chicagoreporter.com, accessed April 25, 2009.

x. The Coiling Feedback Loop of Time

1. "Kelan Phil Cohran," interview by Rebecca Zorach, *Never the Same: Conversations about Art Transforming Politics and Community in Chicago and Beyond* (blog), [2011?], http:/never-the-same.org/interviews/phil-cohran, accessed November 11, 2015.

2. "Afro-Arts Theater May Get License," *Chicago Tribune*, August 4, 1968, https://www.chicagotribune.com, accessed November 11, 2015.

3. "How Chic," *Jet*, May 31, 1973, 40.

4. #TeamEbony, "Lala Anthony Isn't Rushing to Divorce Carmelo Anthony," *Ebony*, June 27, 2017, https://www.ebony.com, accessed February 23, 2021.

5. "Ebony Magazine's New Home," *Ebony*, September 1972, 84-124.

6. Faheem Majeed, unedited interview audiotaped by the author, Chicago, September 2013, for *Reclaimed Soul*, Chicago, Vocalo 91.1FM. Later quotations from Majeed in this chapter are from this interview.

7. Victor Le, personal interview by the author, Chicago, September 2013.

8. Theaster Gates and Jacqueline Najuma Stewart, "DuSable Futures White Paper," Chicago, 2015.

9. Ibid.

10. Dawn Rhodes and Dahleen Glanton, "DuSable Museum Proposal from U. of C. Professor Gets Heated Response," *Chicago Tribune*, July 20, 2015, https://www.chicago tribune.com, accessed August 1, 2015.

11. Gates and Stewart, "DuSable Futures White Paper."

12. Quoted in Rhodes and Glanton, "DuSable Museum Proposal."

13. Ibid.

14. Quoted in Mary Mitchell, "DuSable Museum Fight Exposes Generation Gap," *Chicago Sun-Times*, July 18, 2015, https://chicago.suntimes.com/, accessed August 1, 2015.

15. Mitchell, "DuSable Museum Fight Exposes Generation Gap."

16. Thelma Golden, public speech at Stony Island Arts Bank, Chicago, April 20, 2017 (author attended).

17. Cara Michell, "What the Artist behind Chance the Rapper's Album Art Is Doing for Chicago," *Bloomberg CityLab*, February 12, 2018, https://www.bloomberg.com, accessed February 15, 2021.

18. Brandon Breaux quoted in ibid.

19. John KaSandra, "(What's Under) The Natural Do," Respect Records, 1970, 45 rpm.

20. Dr. Frances Cress Love, public speech at Rainbow PUSH Headquarters, Chicago, October 2017 (author attended).

21. "I'll Write a Song for You," words and music by Philip Bailey, Stephen Beckmeier, and Albert McKay, on *All 'n All* LP, Columbia Records, 1977.

22. Kenneth "Goat" Parks in DeWitt Beall, dir., *Lord Thing*, documentary, 16 mm film, 1970.

23. Julian Reid, personal interview by the author, Chicago, March 2019.

24. For more on bolita, see Kendra Hazen, "Episode 30 Bolita: Bolita and Other Artifacts at Polk County Historical Museum," episode 30, *A History of Central Florida Podcast*, University of Central Florida, 12:24 min., https://stars.library.ucf.edu/, accessed March 15, 2018.

25. For more on St. Clair, see Shirley Stewart, *The World of Stephanie St. Clair: An Entrepreneur, Race Woman, and Outlaw in Early Twentieth Century Harlem* (New York: Peter Lange, 2014).

26. *Valmor Curio Catalog Number 87*, King Novelty Co., 1944, 47.

27. Ibid.

28. *Race, Magic, Mojo: Explorations of Culture, Identity and Spirituality*, symposium PDF, City of Chicago Department of Cultural Affairs, July 24-25, 2015, https://www.chicago .gov, accessed February 25, 2021.

INDEX

INDEX

INDEX

INDEX

AYANA CONTRERAS is a radio host/producer at Chicago Public Media, a founder/blogger at darkjive.com, and a columnist and reviewer at *DownBeat Magazine*.

The University of Illinois Press
is a founding member of the
Association of University Presses.

———————————————

University of Illinois Press
1325 South Oak Street
Champaign, IL 61820-6903
www.press.uillinois.edu